CASCADIA
GARDENING
SERIES

Seasonal Bulbs

Guides for the Northwest Gardener

Ann Lovejoy

SASQUATCH BOOKS
SEATTLE

Printed in the United States of America.

Cover design: Kris Morgan; adapted by Millie Beard
Cover and interior photographs: Mark Lovejoy
Interior design: Lynne Faulk
Garden illustrations: Jean Emmons
Composition: Millie Beard

Library of Congress Cataloging in Publication Data
Lovejoy, Ann, 1951-
  Seasonal Bulbs / Ann Lovejoy.
    p.   cm. — (Cascadia gardening series)
  Includes bibliographical references and index.
  ISBN 1-57061-027-4
  1. Bulbs
     I. Title.   II: Series.
  SB425.L6 1995   94-42438
  635.9'44'09795—dc20   CIP

Sasquatch Books
1008 Western Avenue
Seattle, Washington 98104
(206) 467-4300

Other titles in the Cascadia Gardening Series:
Growing Herbs, by Mary Preus
North Coast Roses, by Rhonda Massingham Hart
Water-Wise Vegetables, by Steve Solomon
Winter Ornamentals, by Daniel Hinkley

Contents

Getting Started with Bulbs

Those of us who garden here in the Pacific Northwest are among the luckiest people on earth. The mild climate allows us to actively pursue our plant passion all year long. True, there are days when even the hardiest of us is driven indoors, but even such days have their compensations. Can anyone really complain about hours spent dreaming over catalogs and nursery lists, making new paper gardens, and rereading our garden journals? Best of all, however, thousands of kinds of plants from all over the temperate world will grow well for us. This emphatically includes bulbs, many of which thrive in our modified Mediterranean climate. Damp, mild winters, extended springs and autumns, and relatively dry summers all favor excellent growth in hundreds of traditional garden bulbs. Indeed, a surprising number of the bulbs we buy from those mail order catalogs actually come from the commercial bulb fields of the maritime Northwest.

Since success with familiar bulbs is almost assured in our gardens, experimenting with less common bulbs is apt to be rewarding as well. As long as we take the time to acquaint ourselves with the specific needs of each new kind we try, we can quite easily expand our plant palettes to include easy-to-please exotics like calla lilies (*Zantedeschia*) and naked ladies (*Amaryllis belladonna*) as well as little-known natives like quamash (*Camassia*).

The best place to start this exciting expansion is with hardy garden bulbs, those that can survive our rare arctic winters without harm. Fortunately, there are enough of these to keep the most ardent of collectors happily trying new ones for many years. Those who want color and fragrance all year round will especially enjoy discovering the hardy off-season bloomers. Hardy cyclamen, cousins of the fat florist's flowers, bloom readily through much of the year. Bright-berried Italian arum

(*Arum italicum* 'Pictum'), with its marbled leaves, and hot pink hardy cyclamen illuminate the solstice. Winter-flowering crocus, saucy winter aconites, and many others join the more familiar snowdrops at the turn of the year.

Although this book is far from comprehensive, it does present a wide range of bulbs, both hardy and tender, that can grow happily in Northwest gardens. While many old favorites are mentioned, I have tried to bring their little-known but worthy relatives to your attention as well. I have also included some wonderful bulbs that are usually grown only by collectors yet could and should be beautifying gardens all over the region. I hope you will find the descriptions of many less familiar bulbs inviting enough to try a few of them. Adding two or three kinds of unfamiliar bulbs each season doesn't cost much, yet it can pay remarkable dividends of pleasure and interest for many years to come.

—*Ann Lovejoy*
Bainbridge Island, Washington

The Bulbs of Spring

CHAPTER 1

March, April, May

Spring brings a heady rush of blossom in its wake. Flowering shrubs cover themselves with glory, precocious perennials are smothered in blossom, and bulbs of all shapes, colors, and sizes burst into ardent bloom. The familiar border tulips and hybrid daffodils need no introduction, but some of their lesser-known relatives do. Dozens of species and hybrids deserve to be more widely grown, for they are just as rewarding as their buxom cousins and far longer lived under the right conditions. Other uncommon bulbs await discovery as well, many of them eager performers with modest cultural requirements. Plump little brown-and-white "mice" (really the inflated blossoms) dive for cover amid the arrow-shaped leaves of mouse plant, *Arisarum probiscideum*. Poppy anemones flower in luxuriant swaths wherever the sun lingers. Scented bulbs abound, from heady true hyacinths to our native trilliums, which release their subtle, wildling fragrance on calm, sunny days.

Here in the maritime Northwest, spring bulbs such as narcissus, which are treated as expensive annuals in many part of the country, return faithfully year after year in gardens where their cultural needs are met. Such ready success means we can also expect great results from many less common bulbs.

The following compendium is by no means complete—an exhaustive list would fill a very fat book indeed. It does, however, offer solid choices that will reward very little effort with exuberant bloom.

ORNAMENTAL SPRING ONIONS (ALLIUM)

Sweetly scented, bright-eyed, and easy to please, ornamental onions effortlessly enliven the spring garden. Nearly all of these early bloomers open hemispherical clusters of small tubular or starry florets above ribbony foliage. Most begin to flower in April, often carrying on into June. Though diminutive in size, they nonetheless put on a bold

1

show, especially when planted in generous quantities. Groups of ten or a dozen make splashy little pools of color throughout the garden. Where space permits, sweeps of a hundred pour in rivers of bloom, scenting the frisky spring breezes and attracting thirsty bees, which hum contentedly at their throats.

Spring onions are perfect plants for young gardens and newer gardeners, for unless planted in a swamp, they never fail to flower. Most will also increase readily, both from seed and by multiplying their bulbs, making gardeners with brown thumbs feel triumphantly successful. Although a few alliums can spread a little too rapidly in open, uncrowded gardens, you can readily control their progress by removing spent flower heads before their seeds ripen or by uprooting the delicate, grassy seedlings if you forget to deadhead in time. In more mature, densely planted gardens, even the most vigorous alliums may dwindle away rather than increase unless they are allowed plenty of elbowroom.

The weirdest and most wonderful of the alliums is among the first to bloom (usually in April and May). *Allium karataviense* (6 inches) spreads its big, broad leaves, slate blue and glittering with a metallic luster, flat upon the ground, interrupted by chubby stalks tipped with globular clusters of wine purple flowers. These are widely separated when they first open, but as the seed heads ripen, the balls compact into solid, shimmering globes of buff and tan that remain attractive for several months after the leaves die off. A tweedy gray carpet of woolly creeping thyme (*Thymus pseudolanuginosus*) makes a handsome backdrop for this delightful allium, and since both enjoy the same conditions, the partnership works well throughout the seasons.

Sunny little *Allium moly* (6 inches) has been a beloved garden plant for centuries, opening golden flowers spangled with lime green, gold-tipped stamens in April and May. It too is a strong grower, spreading in glowing pools of light as a few bulbs expand into colonies. Unimpressive as singletons, these charmers look great in groups, whether encircling deep blue windflowers (*Anemone blanda*) or interplanted with a stand of graceful, white, lily-flowered tulips.

Another heritage plant, *Allium neapolitanum* (6 inches) is a sun-loving southern Italian with slender leaves and green-eyed white flowers like puffs of apple blossom. It revels in an open site, thriving even in poor soils so long as they are well drained. Although it can be crowded out by leafy summer companions, it is an excellent choice for those difficult places where plants with less stamina melt in the heat. It looks especially beautiful planted in snowy sweeps beneath rockroses (*Cistus*), lavender, and bushy sage plants.

The slender, sage green foliage of *Allium oreophilum* (6 inches) shows off its glowing, wine red flowers to a nicety. They open in typical allium fashion, shimmering out of tight-capped buds into loose, hemispherical sprays of rosy blossom in late spring. This little beauty looks smashing beneath black 'Queen of the Night' tulips or intermingled with rosy native *Sedum spathulifolium* and clumps of glossy black mondo grass (*Ophiopogon planiscapus* 'Nigrescens').

Blooming rather late in spring, *Allium unifolium* (to 8 inches) is a sugary confection with satiny foliage—soft green and faintly furred— and rounded clusters of fragrant, cotton candy–pink bells. Groups of tens and twenties look enchantingly pretty dotted between silver-spotted lungworts (*Pulmonaria*) or running in ribbons beneath lacy gray mugworts (*Artemisias*).

PLEASING ALLIUMS: Most spring-blooming alliums share a common desire for sun, space, and well-drained soil. Perennial companions that smother the ground space with thick foliage deprive spring onions of their due and are often the cause when the alliums fail to thrive. Their sun-worshiping ways make them excellent candidates for planting in the hot spots that develop where excess heat and light are reflected off neighboring buildings and streets. Consider them also for sandy seaside gardens, sunny poolsides, and dry sidewalk strips.

With few exceptions, spring alliums grow and flower best when interplanted with shallow-rooted, mild-mannered ground covers. Plants like leadwort (*Ceratostigma plumbaginoides*) or *Vinca minor* 'Miss Jekyll's White' offer little competition for food or water during the bulbs' period of active growth (in winter and spring). These companions are also airy enough in construction that the resting bulbs aren't smothered by their embrace in summer.

WINDFLOWERS (ANEMONE)

The windflower family—which includes herbaceous perennials as well as bulbs and tubers—can keep the garden in color from late winter well into autumn. The Grecian windflower, *Anemone blanda*, is the first to flower, often opening dapper little daisies in late winter along with snowdrops and snow crocus (see Chapter 4, "The Bulbs of Winter").

Flaunting, flame-colored poppy anemone follows rather later, as does the shy wood anemone. Though all are hard workers that perform over several months, their cultural requirements are quite different, so each is discussed individually.

The shape of their roots is equally varied, for some are gnarled tubers, rounded or astonishingly irregular, while others are slender and sticklike. Seeing them, it is hard to imagine that these homely, misshapen lumps can possibly give rise to miraculous beauty, yet happily, such is the case.

Poppy Anemone (*Anemone coronaria*)

Silky, plump-petaled poppy anemones (A. *coronaria*, 10–18 inches) are among my personal favorite flowers, for they manage to be both elegant and opulent at the same time. Indeed, they have been generally admired for centuries, beloved of florists and home gardeners alike. As a result, there are many single color selections to choose from as well as several stunning color mixtures. Their bloom seasons vary by a week or two, but all flower in mid- to late spring, often continuing into early summer.

An old-fashioned strain called 'St. Bavo' (12 inches) produces large, lustrous single blossoms in jewel-toned blues, salmony pinks, rusty and ruby reds, and singing purples, each fringed with thick black stamens at the heart. This strain is rare, and the bulbs are a little tender, so if you manage to find it, grab as many as you can and cherish them, giving them a deep, comfy mulch to get them through the winter. Another British import, the semi-double 'St. Brigid Strain' (12 inches) offers ruffled, many-petaled blooms that look like small peonies in a more typical range of colors, from white through pinks and reds to blues and purples.

Until recently, the Dutch 'Monarch de Caen' hybrids were the biggest and brassiest of the bunch, but a relatively new North American strain called 'Tecolote Giants' (18 inches) has become the new standard. These widely available dazzlers send up sheaves of hand-sized single blossoms from April into June.

If you want to work color magic, try some of the single-color forms like the single, cobalt blue 'Mr. Fokker' or the semi-double, marine blue 'Lord Lieutenant'. 'His Excellency' is a fat, smoldering red single, while 'The Governor' is a sealing wax–red semi-double. Black-eyed, pure-white 'The Bride' is single (though presumably not for long), and 'Mount Everest' is its semi-double counterpart. There are dozens more to seek out in shimmering shades of pink or puce, purple or violet. It doesn't matter much which you try, for all are lovely.

PLEASING POPPY ANEMONES: To please poppy anemones, give them a sunny, protected spot in soil that is well fortified with compost and aged manure, but also well drained (add a good handful of coarse builder's sand if your soil is clay-based). To wake up the slumbering tubers, which are extremely irregular in shape, soak them in warm water for a few hours. Plant them 3–4 inches deep, topping them off with 5–6 inches of mulch to protect them from hard frost. If you can't figure out which way is up, just tuck them in sideways (thinnest side up) and they will straighten themselves out by spring.

Wood Anemone (*Anemone nemorosa*)

When we first came to our present country garden, it was an overgrown mess. Long-abandoned borders had been used as dog runs, and the lawn had reverted to rough meadow. While clearing out brambles and nettles the first spring, we were enchanted to find sheets of white wood anemone, *Anemone nemorosa* (8 inches), threading through the aging shrubbery and spangling the lanky grass. To my delight, they proved to be an unusual heritage form called 'Vestal', with daisylike single petals surrounding tightly quilled centers with tiny, pale gold hearts. Vita Sackville-West adored this little flower, which has never been common, and it was astonishing to find such an abundance of it amid such desolation. Now we have handed great mats of it to various nursery folk, so in time it may be available to anyone who wants it.

Wood anemones are not true bulbs but funny little tubers—long, skinny, and branching like underground twiglets. In their typical species form, they are quietly running plants with leaves like Italian parsley. These emerge in midspring, followed quickly by slender stalks, each tipped with a wide-petaled blossom. The blossoms look much like tiny poppy anemones, though centered with gold fringe instead of black. Most will be white, but blossoms tinged with soft tints of pink or blue are not uncommon.

WOOD ANEMONES IN THE BORDER: Any wood anemone will make an excellent addition to a shady border, for though their wandering roots carry them everywhere, they combine companionably with everything yet harm nothing. Most forms take their time about spreading into pools and rivulets of flowers, but spread they will, so long as they are left undisturbed.

As its name suggests, this pretty runner likes woodsy settings. It grows most ardently in shady gardens, though it is perfectly amenable to morning sun or broken, dappled shade. All forms prefer deep, humus-rich soils that are moist in winter and spring and drier in summer. Wood anemones love the company of rhododendrons and azaleas and wind their way happily between ferns and barrenworts (*Epimedium*). They also make pretty, ruffled skirts that swirl around clumps of dwarf daffodils and scillas under deciduous trees and shrubs.

The natural good looks of the wood anemone make it fit comfortably into shady wildflower gardens. Its elegant simplicity also allows this lovely little flower to keep company with sophisticated companions like black-leaved celandine, *Ranunculus ficaria* 'Brazen Hussy'. Over the centuries, gardeners have selected lots of variations on this typical form, most of them white but some in pink or lavender or blue. Unfortunately, not many of these are readily available, but several regional nurseries offer a few special forms.

William Robinson, father of the naturalistic garden, is commemorated in the chalky blue *Anemone nemorosa* 'Robinsoniana' (8 inches), while the larger, cloud blue 'Allenii' recalls an ardent English gardener of the past century. 'Lismore Blue' and its companion, 'Lismore Pink', have delicately shaded blossoms that gleam shyly through airy nets of miniature *Vinca minor* 'Miss Jekyll's White'. Biggest of all is 'Grandiflora' (10 inches), with flowers the size of a fifty-cent piece. Charming as they all are, my own preference is for oddball forms like the parsley anemone, 'Viridiflora', whose dark green flowers look like Victorian cut lacework, and 'Green Fingers', with long white petals tipped in grassy green.

Jack-in-the-Pulpit (*Arisaema triphyllum*)

When I was a child in New England, I was fascinated by the strange, green-and-brown-striped, hooded flowers of our native Jack-in-the-pulpit, *Arisaema triphyllum*. They often kept company with skunk cabbage, *Symplocarpus foetidus*, in boggy meadows. In gardens, the jaunty Jacks send up their sturdy shoots in midspring, unfurling their striped awnings in slow motion. The flowers fade by midsummer, to be followed by clusters of glistening red berries. Slugs like these too, so you may need to bait around the base of your Jacks in June and July. If you have several plants, they often seed into little colonies, though this is never a rampant plant.

Here in the Northwest, we can enjoy these weird and wonderful plants if we have a shady garden and reasonably moist soil. Though the Jacks and their companion skunk cabbages are at their peak in spring, both have bold foliage that remains attractive for months. Our native Western skunk cabbage, *Lysichiton americanus*, is a handsome substitute for the East Coast version, as is the white-hooded Alaskan, *L. camschatcense*.

Mouse Plant (*Arisarum probiscideum*)

Few plants are cuter than this curious little aroid, which delights the child in everyone. The arrow-shaped leaves cover the ground in shining carpets of deep green. In midspring, the fat little flowers appear, looking exactly like field mice diving for cover amongst the leaves. Pick one and you will find it resembles an inflated sausage casing, creamy white where it rises from its mottled stem and shading abruptly to brown at its midpoint—coloring reminiscent of a brown-and-white field mouse. At its tip, each blossom tapers into a long and curly "tail," which can be 5 to 6 inches long. When a colony is in full bloom, it is these spiraling tails that catch the eye, for one has to look closely to discover the charming mice.

Small enough for the rock garden, *Arisarum probiscideum* (2–3 inches) can be safely encouraged to run through mixed borders, plantings of dwarf shrubs, or woodsy rhododendron gardens. Plant the little tubers about 4 inches below the soil surface, adding a bit of coarse sand or grit to the soil if it is clay-based. Mouse plant grows most luxuriantly in moderately moist, open-textured soils. An annual feeding mulch of compost and aged manure in fall or late winter will increase the size and quantity of fat little flowers. A handful of tubers will become a small colony in just a few seasons, yet this gentle mingler never disturbs its neighbors or needs strict curbing. If you want to divide a group of plants, you can do so in fall as they enter dormancy or in spring when the flowers have faded.

Crocus (*Crocus*)

Dutch or giant crocus, the chubby spring bloomers, need no introduction, for their fat goblets are a familiar sight in nearly every garden.

Like their early-bird cousins, these cheerful charmers bloom soonest in sunny sites. However, the larger crocus also tolerate less-ideal conditions, thriving in almost any kind of soil except a boggy one. Big enough to compete effectively for space, Dutch crocus can easily be naturalized in grass so long as their leaves are allowed to ripen before the surrounding lawn is mown.

When given plenty of room (and not overgrown by companions even when the bulbs are dormant), Dutch crocus often increase quickly, both by seed and by multiplication of their rounded corms. Whether you grow them in beds or borders, group them amid companionable carpets of prostrate ground covers, setting the bulbs in tens and twenties for the fullest effect. These bulbs are so inexpensive that anyone can afford to play around with them to develop satisfying partnerships.

The blue-and-purple-striped 'Pickwick' looks smashing with tidy blue sheep's fescue, *Festuca ovina* 'Blauglut', or rosy native *Sedum spathulifolium* 'Roseum'. Sunny 'Giant Yellow' (probably the most popular crocus in the world) gleams golden against beet-colored bugleweed, *Ajuga reptans* 'Atropurpurea'. 'Giant Yellow' doesn't seed, but it multiplies so fast that a few bulbs quickly become a spreading pool. It's also an early bloomer that frequently begins to flower before winter has faded away, so it's a good one to plant in quantity where winter and spring color is desired.

Avalanche Lily *(Erythronium)*

Our native avalanche lilies are delectable plants, holding their open, reflexed bells above broad, often mottled foliage. In spring, hikers in the Northwestern woods lose their hearts to the tender pink *Erythronium revolutum* (7 inches), its delicate blossoms perfectly set off by silvery patterned leaves. Although there aren't many reputable sources for the species, its lovely form 'Pink Beauty' is fairly easy to locate. So is 'White Beauty', a moon-colored flower that blends beautifully with white violets or provides a satisfying contrast to sea blue scilla or ruffled pink primroses.

California native *E. tuolumnense* (8 inches) offers lemony blossoms that are especially large in the popular hybrid 'Pagoda'. A fast spreader, 'Pagoda' adapts well to various garden conditions. Especially valuable in shady gardens, it runs happily beneath rhododendrons and andromedas, weaving its shining carpets of glossy green leaves and golden flowers.

Avalanche lilies prefer shady spots and open soils with plenty of humus. Give these long-lived plants good company—perhaps the blue lace of our north coast native bleeding heart, *Dicentra formosa* 'Stuart Boothman', or fluffy crested male ferns—that will cover for them during their summer dormancy. Before you plant, think carefully about where you want avalanche lilies. They usually take a season to settle in, but once they do, they resent disturbance and often sulk if moved about too much.

CHECKER LILIES, FRITILLARIES (*FRITILLARIA*)

This big clan includes some fabulous natives as well as exotics from Persia or Kazakhstan or China. Not true lilies, the bell-flowered bulbs range in size from the gigantic crown imperials, which can top 4 feet, to dainty dwarves that need placement in troughs or alpine bulb pans for proper appreciation. They come in many colors, from white or gray to near black, passing through pinks and purples on one side of the family and yellows, tawny oranges, copper, and chocolatey browns on the other.

There are few reputable sources for certain species, which can be tricky to grow well. Because fritillaries (and indeed, many small bulbs) may be endangered in their own habitats, it's important not to buy any that may be collected in the wild rather than nursery-grown. (Good nurseries will gladly tell you where their bulbs are raised.) Happily, the Dutch are doing a good deal of clonal reproduction, so some once rare fritillaries are becoming both widely available and inexpensive.

Despite their reputation for difficulty, plenty of fritillaries are quite easy to grow here in the Northwest. Several delightful species and numerous garden forms are long-lived and apt to increase, if slowly, when their cultural needs are met. All fritillaries can be grown from seed, but the process is lengthy—it can take six or seven years for bulblets to achieve blooming size. Treat yourself to one or two of the following kinds and before long you may find yourself among the plant collectors, eagerly buying any fritillaries you can find.

Crown Imperial (*Fritillaria imperialis*)

Gorgeous, queenly creatures with regal bearing, crown imperials (to 4 feet) are real attention-grabbers when set betwixt more traditional tulips and daffodils. Their single stalks rise from a base of whorled foliage that continues partway up each dark-tinted stem. After a bare stretch of a foot or so, the stalks are tipped with a ruffled topknot of foliage, from which dangle the large, solid-looking bells of red or bitter orange or clean yellow.

Popular in English gardens for four centuries, these strapping beauties are still uncommon on this side of the water. They need not be, for they generally thrive in well-drained soils. Though they flower best in full sun, they will tolerate light or dappled shade, especially when grown in deep, humus-enriched soils.

Crown imperials prefer a site that receives plenty of moisture in winter and spring, when the bulbs are in active growth, yet remains reliably dry during their summer dormancy. To encourage heavier flowering, plant these enormous bulbs at least 6 inches deep (8 inches is even better). Tip the big bulbs on their sides a bit to prevent the crown rots that can develop when rainwater accumulates in the holes left by their drying stems. A handful of coarse grit per bulb will help lighten and open up heavy clay soils, which can also contribute to rot problems.

If your soil is very acid, as native soils so often are in these parts, sprinkle some dolomite garden lime (not the unslaked sort used in outhouses, please) in and around the planting site to sweeten things up a bit. A heaping teaspoon per bulb, well scattered and blended into the entire planting zone, should be sufficient.

Checker Lily *(Fritillaria meleagris)*

These improbable creatures are irresistible to those who love to grow truly unusual plants. Few other flowers boast such regular markings (which really do look like little checkerboards). *Fritillaria meleagris* (12 inches) is usually available in assorted shades—pink-and-purple, cream-and-purple, or green-and-brown checks, with a few solid whites, purples, and rosy pinks thrown in.

Especially good forms, such as the dusky purple 'Saturnus' or warm pink 'Artemis', have been selected for years, but except for the glowing white 'Alba', they are unfortunately rare. However, we can make our own selections by marking bulbs with colors and patterns that appeal to us when in bloom (a bit of yarn, loosely looped about the stem, works well). Carefully separate the chosen plants from their kin after the flowers have faded but before the leaves are dried out. This is how most small bulbs prefer to be moved, so it's a good technique to practice.

Because they are often very dried out when we receive them, and because many of us allow the bulbs to dry out further still while we decide where to put them, fritillaries may fail, or seem to fail at first. Often the real problem is that overly dry bulbs may take several years to recover enough to put on a decent show. It can be a shock to find only a single flower where you planted a dozen bulbs. Indeed, the plants may not appear at all the first year, or only as grassy-looking clumps of thready foliage.

The secret to success is to soak the bulbs for a few hours in warm (never hot) water the day they arrive, then to plant them at once. Checker lilies prefer light or dappled shade and a nutritious, humus-enriched soil. Mark their planting spots well to avoid disturbing them, and then just be patient. Unless you have set them in constantly wet soil, they will eventually come round and produce clusters of curiously patterned bells for many years to come.

Persian Fritillary *(Fritillaria persica)*

Black and glossy-belled, the Persian fritillary (2½ feet) has remained a collector's treasure despite being widely available. This proud beauty deserves to be more frequently grown, for few plants can rival the mysterious enchantment cast by its dusky bells, the pewtery purple petals ghosted with a faint bloom like that on ripe plums.

Persian fritillaries require a warm, sunny spot, preferably sheltered from wind and hard frost by neighboring evergreen shrubs, to give of their best. They enjoy deep, rich soils that are well drained, dry in summer, and moist in winter and spring. A place snug against a south-facing wall can be ideal, particularly if the soil is very free draining.

Widow Iris *(Hermodactylus tuberosus)*

For many years this sleek little iris relative actually was an iris, until those busy taxonomic botanists decreed otherwise. It still looks like an iris, dressed in a fetching floral tuxedo of black and olive green. The somber-sounding color scheme is surprisingly pleasing, especially in contrast to the clear, crayon colors of so many spring bulbs. It looks especially dapper when grown amid creeping thymes, woolly gray or rich green, or the icy blue version of our native *Sedum spathulifolium* 'Capo Blanco'.

Native to southern Europe and the Mediterranean basin, widow iris (*Hermodactylus tuberosus*, 4 inches) demands the usual well-drained, sunny garden spot but is otherwise not picky about soil types. Its long, grassy leaves emerge in fall or early winter, followed in March and April by the funny little flowers. If the bulbs fail to flower, try scattering a bit of diatomaceous earth (or the least toxic slug bait you can find) around the base of the plants, for the plump buds are highly attractive to slugs and snails.

HYACINTHS (*HYACINTHUS ORIENTALIS*)

Swooningly fragrant hyacinths are more often planted in pots than in the garden, yet some of the florist's forcing bulbs prove surprisingly long-lived in borders. A Turkish species, *Hyacinthus orientalis* (10 inches), has given rise to the spectacular forcing and bedding bulbs popularized by Dutch breeders. Nearly all will reappear for many seasons when given ordinary garden situations. Decent soil, a reasonable amount of sun, and an annual mulching of compost and aged manure in fall will keep them coming back dependably.

The first year's flowers are always the showiest. In later years, the looser, slightly smaller flower heads that appear are less artificial looking and seem more in harmony with the natural graces of companions like wood anemones and species daffodils. Try pairing white 'L'Innocence' and deep sea blue 'Blue Jacket' with lemony daffodils, or mingle chalky 'City of Haarlem' and peachy apricot 'Gypsy Queen' with 'Apricot Beauty' tulips and pale yellow 'Moonlight' broom for a truly memorable combination. An antique double-flowered variety, 'Hollyhock', has flowers of deep rosy red that make exceptional partners for clumps of black mondo grass, *Ophiopogon planiscapus* 'Nigrescens'.

Grape Hyacinth (*Muscari*)

Sweetly scented and eager to multiply, grape hyacinths are tough survivors, often persisting in old gardens after long years of neglect. The most common species, *Muscari armeniacum* (6 inches), is a delightful pest in some gardens, for its take-over tendencies can be hard to curb. Its celeste blue spikes are pretty in March and April, but the lush, lank foliage is rank by summer. Indeed, the flopsy foliage makes grape hyacinth both unsightly and unsafe for smaller companions, which can easily be smothered beneath the weight of those thready leaves.

One solution is to chop the foliage back hard when it begins to flop (usually in May or June). This deters the bulb a little, but that's not a bad thing. Another solution is to use these cheerful charmers in places where their wandering ways won't cause heartache. Woodsy wild gardens, rhododendron ghettos, and stately shrub borders are all improved by a lacing of brilliant blue ribbons in spring. Don't, however, put grape hyacinth in the rock garden or you will be pulling it out for years to come.

Several related grape hyacinths have better manners and can be safely invited into the border. Bicolored *Muscari latifolium* (6 inches) is a two-tone job with lake blue tips above marine blue bases. It has broader leaves, somewhat like tulip foliage, and although it will increase nicely, it is never naughty. The feather hyacinth, M. *comosum* 'Plumosum' (5 inches), is a slower grower with fluffy, violet blue flowers that are starry rather than bell-like. A hybrid called 'Blue Spike' has Delft blue blossoms that are fatly doubled and very showy in clumps. This one is sterile and rather slow to increase, as is dainty, white-belled M. *botryoides* 'Album'.

Even the less rampant grape hyacinths need very little encouragement, which makes them excellent first bulbs for the advancing neophyte. Unless planted in soggy soil or dank shade, all will reliably reappear and increase. To divide a colony or clump, wait until the flowers fade, then dig it up while the leaves are still green. Split the tightly packed bulbs into smaller groups and set these around golden forsythia or a yellow-leaved mock orange (*Philadelphus coronarius* 'Aureus') for a spectacular display.

DAFFODILS (NARCISSUS)

The sight of golden daffodils tossed by the soft chinook wind is as familiar as the face of spring itself. If ordinary daffodils such as yellow 'King Alfred' or white 'Mount Hood' thrill your spirit, some major treats are in store as you explore the diversity of this exceptional clan. Try pairing 'Cloud Nine', a reverse bicolor with a cloudy white trumpet surrounded by a ruff of sunny yellow, with its opposite number, 'Magnet', whose straight yellow skirt is encircled by creamy petals. Round as a cookie, 'Modern Art' has overlapping, hot yellow outer petals around a ruffled, deep orange heart, its trumpet converted to a frou-frou dance skirt. 'Professor Einstein' is a compact, restrained white with a flaring, dark orange trumpet, while 'Scarlett O'Hara' is appropriately outsized, a dazzler with soft yellow petals around a fluted trumpet of muted orange.

Once a rare novelty, pink daffodils are becoming relatively common. The split-cup 'Palmares' is one of the prettiest, with pointed white petals centered by a froth of foamy pink lace. 'Petit Four' is as confectionary as it sounds, its icing-white petals enclosing a sugary pink heart that looks like a small carnation. 'Filly' is simple in form, with slightly reflexed cream petals folding back from a peachy pink trumpet, while seductive 'Salome' has an apricot trumpet that ripens to shell pink amid pleated white petals.

Daffodils bloom well in full or partial sun, generally enjoying a long, productive life under ordinary garden conditions. Tolerant, they will often increase in nearly any decent soil that is reasonably well drained and sufficiently nourishing without being overly rich. Heavy, severely acid Northwest clays should be amended with dolomite lime (see Chapter 7, "Practical Pointers") to bring the soil pH closer to neutral. Spring and fall mulches of compost and aged manure will usually provide plenty of nutrition, but a commercial bulb food can be added where soils are lean or poor.

Poet's Narcissus (Narcissus poeticus)

Few flowers can rival this late-blooming species, which is often found naturalized around older gardens or homesteads throughout the Northwest. Narcissus poeticus (14 inches) produces long, slim foliage and many small white flowers in May and June, each centered with a tiny, golden-eyed cup rimmed in ruby. From them we drink not nectar but an enticing floral fragrance that smells like the breath of spring, at once heady and innocent.

Fine-textured as raw silk, the poet's narcissus is as satisfying to touch as to see, so it's especially nice that the flowers last well when cut. Several named forms are widely available, including the large-flowered 'Actea' and one with especially reflexed petals called 'Recurvus'. Unlike most narcissus, the poets prefer dampish (but never boggy) soils and full sun or dappled shade.

Wake-Robin (Trillium)

The splayed, three-petaled blossoms of the wake-robin, Trillium ovatum (to 14 inches), are a common sight in Northwestern woods, where they may come into flower as early as February and continue into April. A plant of threes, its three petals are offset by the three green wings of the calyx, while just below them spread three broadly lobed leaflets that spring stemless from the mottled stalk. Glossy, rippling, and richly green, the leaves are among the loveliest in the family, making the Western trillium a better garden choice (to my mind, anyway) than the more popular Eastern version, *T. grandiflorum*.

Natural woodlanders, trilliums grow happily in shady or wild gardens, enjoying the same conditions that please rhododendrons and azaleas. Deep, open soils, well amended with humus and evenly moist in winter and spring but rather drier in summer, will suit them down to the ground. However, it's important to resist the temptation to move mature plants from their native woods to the garden, or even to detach offsets from large plants. Not only do they rarely survive the transition, but the mother plants are often killed as well. Only when the bulldozers are in sight is it acceptable practice to move wild plants, which are daily dwindling, thanks to the depredations of spreading suburbia.

Since trilliums are so easily grown from seed, it's best to either grow your own or buy from reputable sources. Happily, there are many such in our region, some of which offer interesting variant forms with rosy or green flowers as well as doubled or hose-in-hose (flower-within-a-flower) blossoms. Mottled trillium, *T. chloropetalum*, is another native beauty with gorgeously patterned leaves and closed, shuttlecock flowers that may be creamy or soft yellow, or various shades of pink and purple-red. Darker in leaf and flower is *T. sessile*, a Northeasterner with dim red flowers and truly splendid foliage. Pair any of these with wood anemones and lungworts (*Pulmonaria*) for lovely, long-lasting spring combinations.

TULIPS (*TULIPA*)

Although they're every bit as popular as daffodils, it's rare to find tulips surviving, let alone naturalized, in older gardens. In part, this reflects their more exotic origins. Many daffodils come from the Mediterranean basin, where climates and weather patterns are not dissimilar to those of the maritime Northwest. Most tulips hail from the steppes of Uzbekistan or the roof of the world, wild passes of remote mountain ranges like the Pakistani Karakoram and the Himalayas. There, winters and summers are equally fierce, providing a range of temperature and weather conditions we can't hope to match in our home gardens.

Most of us resolve this dilemma by treating tulips as expensive annuals (or deluxe treats for resident mice). However, given deep planting (8-10 inches), well-drained soil, and as much sun as we can muster, quite a few border tulips can be persuaded to return for at least a few years. The kind sold as "single early tulips" (to 14 inches), such as 'Princess Irene' (copper red flamed with green and orange) and cherry red 'Couleur Cardinal', can be remarkably persistent, as may certain of the big-blossomed Darwins (to 26 inches), such as midnight-colored 'Black Diamond' or single late, white 'Maureen'.

Longest-lived of all are the botanical tulips, a group of early-flowering species and simple hybrids. The lady tulip, or peppermint stick (*Tulipa clusiana*, to 12 inches), is the most graceful, slim and upright, its white petals licked with red on the outside and wine-stained at the heart. The beautiful tulip *T. pulchella* 'Violacea' (5 inches) looks like a miniature version of the border queens, with chubby buds that open into rosy, rounded cups. Apricot pink *T. batalini* 'Bronze Charm' (5 inches) turns from pointed rosebuds into coppery little goblets that glimmer delightfully against brighter oranges, dull reds, or smoky purples.

Earliest to bloom in my garden is the Russian *T. tarda* (4 inches), a cheerful dwarf with pointed ivory petals liberally splashed with yolk yellow. In sunny weather they are open-hearted, but they close up tightly on cloudy days, showing backs marked with murky lavender-green. Similar in coloration but quite different in form, delicate *T. turkestanica* (7 inches) holds its starry, golden-hearted white flowers in small sprays above handsome, sea green leaves.

All of these small tulips share an appreciation for sunny sites and open, fast-draining soils that are neutral or slightly acid. Most will thrive in border settings so long as they are not crowded out by summer-flowering companions. If allowed to thoroughly ripen their foliage (which is relatively unobtrusive), many will seed and proliferate by bulblets (or pups, as they are sometimes called) into pools and broad ribbons throughout the garden.

The Bulbs of Summer

CHAPTER 2

June, July, August

Summer's riches are all but unending as bulbs and their perennial companions bloom in sequential sweeps from early June right into autumn. Summer onions open the season, their rounded or dangling heads spangled first with flowers, then with glossy seeds. Lilies arrive in force by midsummer, and a well-chosen selection will carry on for a couple of months. Spiky gladiolas, dangling angels' fishing rods (*Dierama*), stalwart crocosmias, and dappled tiger flowers (*Tigridia*) follow each other in the dance, each taking the lead in turn. Lilies-of-the-Nile (*Agapanthus*) explode like floral fireworks above their strappy foliage. A Chinese Jack-in-the-pulpit, *Arisaema candidissimum*, unfurls its pale, pink-striped spathe between enormous, fatly lobed leaves. True lilies spill their heady scents, while evening-fragrant species gladiolas glow in silvery moonlight, filling the warm summer nights with the breath of romance.

SUMMER ORNAMENTAL ONIONS (ALLIUM)

When I was an impressionable teenager, I saw in an English garden a plant combination that seemed the essence of romance. A low, sprawling rosebush, smothered beneath its pale pink foam of flowers, was heavily underplanted with graceful, nodding sprays of ivory blossoms that looked like tiny, fairy-sized lilies. To my delight, the rose was a dwarf polyantha called 'The Fairy'. It was, however, a bit shattering to learn that the enchanting little lilies were actually onions. It seemed impossible—how could such sweetly scented, delicately shaped flowers be something so prosaic as onions?

I soon learned that onions belong to the lily family and that many of them are held in high horticultural standing. Although the fairy lilies that captured my young heart were charming Cinderellas, whisked from the dull kitchen garden to queen it in the border (they were Chinese chives, *Allium tuberosum*), some of their more glamorous cousins have never been expected to do kitchen duty at all.

As we have seen, quite a handful of cute little spring onions bloom along with more traditional bulbs. However, certain summer onions rank among the showiest flowers in the garden, holding their own even against the roses and rodgersias or daylilies and dahlias. Like kitchen onions, they prefer sunny, open sites and decent garden soils, rich but well drained. They need adequate moisture to bloom well, but live longest and perform best where they do not receive excess summer water. (This makes them natural candidates for dry or low-water gardens.)

Ornamental onions are good minglers, requiring very little ground space but expanding rapidly to fill in gaps between neighbors. The taller onions create fascinating aerial displays that can pull the eye from sagging companions. Nearly all are happy to be interlayered with other bulbs, making it easy to create colorful, multiseasonal garden arrangements. Most of them are as handsome in seed head as in flower, remaining decidedly ornamental for months. In winter, the seed heads detach and blow about like little tumbleweeds, seeding themselves into all sorts of interesting places. If you don't want them, the seedlings are easy to weed out, but such freely offered placement suggestions (which are often brilliant and uncommon) are always worth considering.

In my garden, the first of the summer onions appears in May, when the stout stalks and broad, fuzzy gray leaves of *Allium* 'Purple Sensation' (to 30 inches) rise above the surrounding foliage. By mid-May, the fat buds have split their tight sheaths, opening into stunning, softball-sized globes studded like pomander balls with hot, bright purple florets. They hold their color until late June, when they begin to fade and bleach. As August draws near, they are still going strong, though looking positively Martian, like little spaceships that have wandered into the border.

Another May and June bloomer, *A. christophii* (to 3 feet), is rather similar but built on a larger scale. Packed with metallic, twilight purple florets, the heads can be 10 inches or more across. They look super lurking beneath the dusky skirts of the purple-leaved *Rosa rubrifolia* or matching blues with the non-climbing navy blue *Clematis* × *durandii*. In July, *Allium giganteum* comes into bloom. This outsized creature can reach 5 feet in height when well pleased. Its enormous flower heads are the size of grapefruit, their florets a rich violet. Such big plants need plenty of room and look most dramatic when planted in odd-numbered groups between leafy companions. Space them a good 18 inches apart, then stand back; they grow fast.

My personal favorite is both the weirdest and the most spectacular of the summer onions. Long a rare collector's plant, A. *schubertii* is beginning to turn up in nurseries and catalogs. Though its stems are relatively short (to 2 feet), its flower heads are as big as basketballs, pale pinky purple and spangled with silver gray. Instead of being densely packed balls, the flower heads hold sprays and spurts of florets all blossoming at varying heights. Some are short-necked; others stretch a good 8–10 inches from the stem, creating a gauzy effect that remains enchanting long after the color drains away. That takes some time, for this one often holds its color from June well into August.

Jack-in-the-Pulpit *(Arisaema candidissimum)*

A stunning Chinese Jack-in-the-pulpit, *Arisaema candidissimum*, opens its creamy, pink-and-green-striped flower head (technically a spathe) in June. Tight, fat buds swell into silky monks' hoods, each with a slim green spike (spadix) inside. These are soon followed by enormous leaves with three large lobes, bold enough in size and form to balance big hostas and cascading grasses like *Hakonechloa macra* 'Aureola'. Like most Jack-in-the-pulpits, it is surprisingly easy to please so long as its roots are not allowed to dry out. In moist situations, it grows happily in full sun. Otherwise, a leafy mulch and humus-rich soil in light or partial shade will encourage it to spread and seed into little colonies.

Because A. *candidissimum* is a late riser, showing no sign of bud or leaf until early June, it is vital that its resting place be marked in some way. Otherwise, a hasty shovel ("Here's an empty spot where I can jam in this new fern!") can easily destroy the fragile storage tuber. Circles of small stones, short bamboo canes, and permanent (metal) garden labels are all discreet marking methods that won't offend the eye while the plants are dormant.

Blue Dick *(Brodiaea)*

The woods and hills of California are blue with these cheerful, spiky wildflowers, first in early spring and again in summer when the harvest brodiaeas bloom. Little known outside of the West Coast, these fetching creatures deserve wider circulation, for the family is a charming one. Over the years, the brodiaeas have been lumped and split by botanists, so they are sometimes found listed as *Triteleia, Dichelostemma,*

Ipheion, or any of several other things. However you find them, all are well worth growing wherever they are hardy.

Most commonly available is the very hardy *Brodiaea* (or *Triteleia*) *laxa* (2 feet), which produces its warm blue blossoms in June. Showier and longer in bloom, 'Queen Fabiola' (to 2½ feet) is a midsummer bloomer that produces fat little umbels of cupped bell flowers in saturated violet blue. The thready, fine-textured foliage is usually fading when the flowers peak, so it's best to give the queen a suitable consort. A carpet of crinkled black spinach bugleweed (*Ajuga pyramidalis* 'Metallica Crispa') or the prostrate form of our native beach wormwood, *Artemisia stelleriana* 'Silver Brocade', will set off her sapphires to a nicety.

Camas, Quamash *(Camassia)*

Northwestern natives, *Camassia quamash* (18–30 inches) are edible, onionlike bulbs that early settlers reported eating with salmon and blackberries in what sounds like a local form of chutney. The flowers appear in soft spires, the stamen-spangled, starry florets opening from the bottom up and twisting upright as they mature. Oregonian *C. leichtlinii* 'Alba' (2–3 feet) is a lovely white camas, while *C. cusickii* (to 2 feet) is a delicate lavender blue.

In the wild, camas pour through moist Northwestern meadows in living streams and pools of vivid blue. As their natural habitats disappear beneath the bulldozer, it behooves us to grow these beautiful bulbs in our gardens wherever we can. Cloned bulbs—mostly European imports—may be bought from specialty nurseries; as is so often the case, our native plants have long been admired abroad while getting little recognition at home.

Collecting plants in the wild is rarely a good idea, but it is definitely worth seeking permission to dig them up where land is slated for development. Indeed, camas bulbs look beautiful in natural meadow gardens and are better suited to our maritime climate than the Midwestern prairie dwellers found in the usual meadow seed mixes. Wild camas is too rare to eat these days, but if you are tempted, be very sure you are not munching on death camas, *Zigadenus elegans*, which looks very similar to the benign *C. quamash*.

Montbretia *(Crocosmia)*

Huge clumps of montbretia, or *Crocosmia masonorum* (to 4 feet), are often found in older gardens, their irislike clumps spreading implacably despite weeds and neglect. Their horizontally held, open spikes of volcanic orange, tubular flowers are less attractive than those of more recent hybrids, some of which are dazzling enough to stop traffic when they bloom in high summer. Blazing red 'Lucifer' (5 feet) is one such, as is coppery-red-and-burnt-orange 'Firebird' (4½ feet), sprays of which look like tropical birds in flight. Both have superb foliage that spreads in majestic fans above lesser plants.

There are numerous exciting forms to try if you prefer smaller-scale plants. 'Emily McKenzie' (to 2 feet) is a late-summer bloomer whose exceptionally large, tomato orange blossoms are splotched at the throat with chocolate. 'Norwich Canary' (2 feet) has chartreuse foliage and canary yellow flowers, while 'Citronella' has deeper foliage and clearer yellow blossoms. Favorite of colorists, the stunning 'Solfaterre' (2 feet) offers smoky copper foliage and deep apricot flowers.

All grow well in sunny gardens, adapting cheerfully to nearly any soil. When hard winters threaten, a thick layer of mulch will bring the bulbs through without harm. Where happy, the bulbs multiply quite quickly. If mature clumps begin to bloom sparsely, split them into several groups and they will recover their vigor.

Angels' Fishing Rod, Wandflower *(Dierama)*

I first saw this remarkable plant growing between paving stones on a prim English terrace. I hardly noticed the leathery, swordlike leaves, for what caught my attention were soft clusters of sweet-pea–pink bell flowers dangling on whippy, flexuous stems just above my head. They do, indeed, look like angels' bait, for *Dierama pulcherrimum* (to 7 feet) has an ethereal, unworldly quality about it. A number of pretty forms are available in more sweet-pea colors, from syrupy purple through sugary pinks to near-white, all of which bloom in early summer. Similar but more compact, Wandflower, *D. pendulum* (4–6 feet), blooms a bit earlier and is more prone to winter damage.

Both luscious confections enjoy full sun and tolerate dry soils, but prefer plenty of water when in active growth. Even a few corms will form a large plant in time, but mature clumps deeply resent disturbance, so do not divide them lightly. Although evergreen, the leaves look decidedly worse for wear by spring. Cut old leaves back hard, and by bloom time, the plants will be refurbished. A deep mulch will reduce wind and frost damage in hard winters.

Voodoo Lily *(Dracunculus vulgaris)*

Mysterious and bizarrely beautiful, the Mediterranean voodoo lily (*Dracunculus vulgaris*, to 36 inches) adapts remarkably well to warmer maritime gardens. It especially thrives in windswept, seaside sites, keeping company with the rock roses (*Cistus* spp.) and evergreen perennial herbs that accompany it in its native habitat. Lavender, rosemary, and sage are all great partners for this tropical-looking bulb. It sends up a stout, dappled stalk in midspring, unfurling great, elegantly divided leaves a few weeks later. These are followed in early summer by astonishing 18-inch flowers (spathes) resembling medieval hoods—long, tapered, and midnight red, each centered with a skinny black wand (spadix).

As its Latin name suggests, this gorgeous plant has its vulgar side, for when the blossom first opens, it releases a truly repugnant scent of rotting flesh. This vile habit does have a purpose—it serves to attract its pollinators, insects that feed on carrion—and fortunately the smell lasts only for a day or two. Just don't plant one right beside the picnic table or under the kitchen window (you might find yourself ignoring the dirty dishes for a few days in June). Despite this unattractive trait, this splendid plant is well worth growing, as much for its exceptionally beautiful leaves as for the murky, magical flowers.

GLADIOLAS (*GLADIOLUS*)

Most gardeners are familiar with the brilliant hybrid gladiolas sold as annual bulbs. Some are indeed delightful creations, striking in coloring and stiffly architectural in form. Most are too individualistic and highly colored to meld well in borders; the best are better mixers, and a few groups of ten or a dozen of these make interestingly ruffled tiers above waves of less structural plants. Smoky lavender-and-mauve 'Zigeunerbaron' is a delicious blender with purples and pinks, as is the tender pink 'Rose Supreme'. Both the dusky, mysteriously dark 'Blue Bird' and the intensely purple 'Plumtart' will highlight chartreuse and old gold or stronger, clarion yellows with panache. Lemon-hearted 'White Friendship' is an older hybrid that has never been surpassed; it sparkles amid the gilded leaves and small white daisies of golden feverfew and the summer-sky–colored cornucopias of 'Heavenly Blue' morning glories.

Although many hybrid gladiolas are not winter-hardy and require lifting (see Chapter 6, "Bulbs in Containers"), quite a few will winter over with ease. In mild years, a dozen bulbs left in the ground may reappear redoubled come spring. It's always worth trying, for they are inexpensive enough to replace freely if the experiment fails.

Hardy Species Gladiolas

Less familiar are the hardy species gladiolas, of which only a handful are widely available. A sultry Mediterranean, *Gladiolus byzantinus* (to 30 inches), is sometimes sold at bargain prices through general nursery catalogs. Its hot purple-red flowers are most aptly called magenta but are usually referred to as rosy purple, since so many people shy away from the former word (even though they often love the color itself). Whatever name you give its tint, if you partner it with gray and silver, the rose-and-purple G. *byzantinus* becomes a glowing marvel, looking like stained glass when it catches slanting morning or evening light. If you can find it, the white form, 'Albus', is easily incorporated into pastel color schemes. A strong, adaptable grower, G. *byzantinus* is very hardy when grown in full sun and well-drained soil.

Long sold as *Acidanthera murielae*, *Gladiolus bicolor* 'Murielae' (2–3 feet) is a splendid creature, with large, irregularly shaped flowers arching on elongated, cylindrical necks from tall, sturdy stems. The intensely fragrant white flowers are strongly splashed with circles of inky purple at their throats, making what is called an eye-zone of subfusc color. Swordlike leaves marked with neat, longitudinal pleats give this species additional value as a foliage plant.

Gladiolus nanus

The hardy, diminutive hybrids offered as forms of G. *nanus* (to 15 inches) are midsummer bloomers, usually sold in time for autumn rather than spring planting. They are most often available as a mixture of warm and pastel colors, but sometimes individual forms can be found. These are softer in form than the big hybrids, with airy sprays of small flowers on arching stems. Perhaps the best is vivacious, lipstick-red 'Amanda Mahy', a stellar companion for the chalky yellow flowers of *Dianthus knappii* and the coppery foliage of native coral bells, *Heuchera americana*. 'The Bride' (actually a form of G. *colvillei*) has starry white flowers with lemon-lime hearts and a delicate fragrance. It is more tender than the others and needs a thick winter mulch.

Sad Glads

Understated and elegant, the sinuous, swaying stalks of G. *papilio* (to 4 feet)—sometimes called "the sad glad"—carry swags of ivory bells in late summer. Each heavy bell is marked on the inside with two great, green teardrops edged with smoky purple smudges. This romantic creature self-sows with abandon, or perhaps the birds carry it about, for it wanders through the garden, always lending itself to stunning combinations. In my garden, a dozen stalks rise between a gilded *Spiraea japonica* 'Gold-flame' and the black lace leaves of a bugbane, *Cimicifuga ramosa* 'Atropurpurea'. Several times *Gladiolus papilio* has put itself into the lower branches of purple beautyberry, *Callicarpa bodinieri* var. *giraldii* 'Profusion', to splendid effect. It also looks remarkably nice spurting up through the hazy blue lacecaps of *Hydrangea macrophylla* 'Mariesii' or 'Blue Wave'.

Pallid, fragrant *Gladiolus tristis* (to 24 inches) boasts narrow white blossoms with burgundy and lemon stippling inside. Although the Latin name *tristis* means sad or sorrowful, this is a cheerful little thing with a powerful if intermittent fragrance. It smells especially sweet on overcast days—a distinct advantage here in the maritime Northwest. Most reliably fragrant during the evenings, G. *tristis* is a great candidate for a moon garden. (Moon gardens hold pale, light-reflective flowers, often night-fragrant, which look lovely by moonlight.)

Native to the Cape of South Africa, G. *tristis* prefers moister soils than most gladiolas. In colder, open gardens, the bulbs require winter protection such as deep mulch, clear plastic greenhouse umbrellas or a small cloche, or lifting and storage (see Chapter 6, "Bulbs in Containers," for more details on winter protection).

All of the hardy gladiolas grow best in nutritious, well-drained garden soils, well amended with grit or coarse sand in the case of heavy clays. Most prefer a situation in full sun, although G. *papilio* often sows itself into half shade and grows happily there.

LILIES (*LILIUM*)

Lilies are the stars of the high summer garden. Fragrant, graceful, vigorous, and beautiful, they thrive wherever their simple needs—plenty of light (not always direct sunlight), good air circulation, and excellent drainage—are met. Nearly all appreciate a steady supply of moisture when in active growth, usually from early spring into summer, but very few can tolerate soggy or stagnant soils.

Most lily bulbs look fairly similar—large, roughly egg-shaped, and wrapped with soft, overlapping scales—but it is important to know at planting time whether they are stem rooters or not. Many of the most common lilies are stem-rooting, which means that after the bulb is planted, it produces feeding roots both from the flat, rounded area on its bottom (the basal plate) and along the first few inches of stem. Naturally enough, such bulbs require deep planting, at least six inches below the soil surface, so that the feeder roots can gather nutrients. Stem rooters also prefer deep but open-textured mulches; a mixture of chopped leaves and coarsely shredded bark is ideal.

Lilies that are not stem-rooting have different needs, and won't perform well if planted or mulched too deeply. Since some of these are especially good garden plants in the maritime Northwest, it is worth seeking them out and learning to please them, for they can bring great beauty to the garden and pleasure to the gardener. The most important of these are the lovely Madonna lilies—which are widely available—and a less well known group of hybrids developed in Bellingham, Washington, from various North American species. The Bellingham hybrids are terrific garden plants and can be found in the catalogs of several regional bulb growers.

Here in the Northwest, gardeners with loamy, sand-based soils often enjoy the most lasting success with lilies. All they need do is plant their bulbs with ordinary care and enjoy the subsequent flowers. Indeed, in favored sites, many lilies will multiply into colonies that can be divided every five or six years, the excess bulbs shared with friends or reset in groups around the garden.

For these lucky folks, the key to success with lilies is allowing the stems and foliage to ripen and turn brown before tidying them away. Unless you want to try your hand at hybridizing, it's a good idea to clip off the tops of each stalk once the flowers are spent. This directs the plant's energy down to the roots so that it is stored in the bulbs rather than expended in seed production. It's fine to trim the stems away a few inches at a time as they brown off, but don't rush the process by removing green foliage or stems.

GROWING LILIES IN CLAY SOILS: Those who garden on heavy clay-based soils may feel that lilies are expensive annuals, for without quick drainage, bulbs dwindle or rot away in wet winters. The solution is either to grow our lilies in pots, where the soil mix can be carefully controlled, or to give them generous planting holes, at least 18 inches deep. If you do this, fill the bottom third with grit or coarse builder's sand (not fine-textured sandbox sand, which turns clay into adobe or brick). Next add 6 inches of aged manure and compost, then spoon in more sandy grit and stir this top layer together without disturbing the sand beneath. Before setting the bulbs, top this mixture with another few inches of grit. Nestle the bulbs into this, top them off with a gritty blend of compost and sand, and mulch the planting area with coarsely shredded bark. This way, the bulbs are sitting on a bed of sand, yet their roots can easily reach the humus-laden nutritional layer of soil.

Regal Lily

One of the most willing workers in any soil or situation is the regal lily, *Lilium regale* (3–4 feet). Not only is it tolerant of heavy clay soils, it does as well in sun as in light or dappled shade. Regal lilies look something like Easter lilies, but rather taller. Their long, purple-stained buds open into glowing white goblets spilling with golden pollen that stains your nose for days if you drink too deeply of its intoxicating scent. Regal lilies come quickly from seed, reaching blooming size in just two or three years, so it's easy to have plenty of them around. They look wonderful massed beneath dark-leaved *Rosa rubrifolia* or a purple smoke bush like *Cotinus coggygria* 'Royal Purple' or 'Velvet Cloak'.

Asiatic Lily

Almost equally durable are the Asiatic hybrids (28–40 inches), shorter lilies with starry, upfacing flowers clustered atop compact stems. Tolerant of most soil conditions (except soggy ones), Asiatics appreciate plenty of sun but benefit from light midday shade in hot situations such as reflective patios and poolsides. They bloom in June and July, often for five or six weeks at a stretch. Lovely and long-lasting both as cut flowers and in the border, they lack only scent to make them sublime garden plants.

Some of the newest Asiatics sold as "pot lilies" are sadly ill-proportioned, graceless and squatty, with overly large flowers on stumpy stems. Those with smaller flowers, such as the hot orange 'Enchantment', with paprika-colored freckles, look far less awkward. 'Enchantment'—the very first of the Asiatics to be named—has been enormously popular for decades, but there are dozens more to choose amongst, from moonlight-pale 'Roma', with a texture of heavy silk, to the strawberries and cream of 'Unique' or the golden amber cups of 'Dreamland'. One of my favorites, 'Red Night', is midnight red with black freckles, an exceptional partner for purple sage (*Salvia officinalis* 'Purpurascens') and red castor beans (*Ricinis communis* 'Carmencita').

A second group of Asiatics is classified as outward-facing, since the flower stems are set at a lower (more nearly horizontal) angle. Some gardeners prefer this shyer look, which is closer to the natural, nodding grace of many species lilies. Prettiest among these are delicate 'Pink Butterflies', with palest shell pink blossoms lightly freckled with plum, and 'George Slate', with airy, curling blossoms the color of candlelight or fresh butter, each petal lightly peppered with tiny beauty marks. Both prefer light or dappled shade, but the tall, sumptuously colored 'Red Velvet' flaunts its subtle, shifting shades of red in full sun. 'Citronella', with gentle yellow flowers that quiver at the least breeze, and glowing yellow 'Last Dance' both thrive in sun or light shade.

Bellingham Hybrid

Bred from a group of native Northwestern lilies, the Bellingham hybrids (and the related San Juan strain) are vigorous, healthy-looking plants, tall and branching and spangled with reflexed, curling flowers that resemble martagon or Turk's-cap lilies (*Lilium martagon*). Most of them boast smallish, heavily speckled flowers in deep shades of yellow and orange with a few good pinks and rusty or cinnamon reds. Not stem rooters, these showy bulbs prefer shallow planting in moist, open-textured soils with plenty of humus. They do best in light or dappled shade, and can greatly enliven our stolid rhododendron and azalea ghettos in high summer. Any of the parent species (mostly *L. pardalinum*, *L. parryi*, and *L. humboldtii*) are worth seeking out as well, and all will enjoy similar conditions.

Madonna Lily *(Lilium candidum)*

Madonna lilies, *Lilium candidum* (to 5 feet), with their trumpeting form, satiny, pure-white petals, and a swooningly pretty scent, have been beloved garden plants since the time of Theseus. Unlike most lilies, Madonna lilies prefer shallow planting; their tips should rest just below the soil surface, and they should not be mulched too deeply. As soon as they are planted in early autumn, the bulbs begin to produce little tussocks of foliage that remain green all winter. These resting rosettes must not be smothered, so don't worry about frostbite, but mulch them lightly and make sure they get plenty of light and air.

Madonna lilies prefer sunny, well-drained garden spots, sheltered from wind by neighboring shrubs or house walls. They don't mind having their lower stems shaded by companion plants, but they like to stretch their long necks up into the sun. They will even thrive in downright hot situations where most lilies would sizzle, so consider these graceful creatures for poolside plantings, near patios and walkways, and on sunny banks or berms.

Less thirsty than most lilies, Madonnas prefer modest amounts of water in spring and early summer and enjoy the same summer baking they received in their native Mediterranean habitat. (When we speak of bulbs liking a summer baking, it means they do well in a south-facing position, not that they actually want to be cooked. In totally waterless situations, even sun lovers may look stressed and unhappy.)

Trumpet Lily

Showiest of the lilies are the splendid trumpets, tall and brazen, spilling their rich golden pollen as freely as their intoxicating scent. Trumpet lilies are complex hybrids that are available both as seed strains (which means the plants will be variable) and as named clones, which should all be identical to the original plant. Seed-grown plants often mature quickly and are usually relatively inexpensive. Clones that increase quickly may be similarly reasonable, while slow increasers (or very rare bulbs) may be dear indeed. This is why seed-grown bulbs of the famous 'Black Dragon' trumpet strain cost a mere three or four dollars apiece, while a clone of the original mother bulb will run ten times that. Fortunately, some of the most gorgeous clones cost no more than seedlings, so we can indulge in all our favorite colors without feeling too extravagant.

PLEASING TRUMPET LILIES: Trumpet lilies are stem rooters that appreciate deep, rich, yet well-drained soils and plenty of light. The gentler colors fade in strong sun but develop marvelously in dappled shade or half sun (direct morning light is better than midday or afternoon sun). All colors hold their bloom longer and in better condition in light, high shade than in full sun. The bulbs will benefit from a thick mulch, which conserves moisture and keeps the soil temperature cooler in hot weather. Late bloomers, trumpets carry on from late

June into August, lasting longest when given moderate amounts of summer water—delivered to the roots, rather than sprinkled onto blossom-laden stems.

Because they can become very tall when well grown (a happy 'Black Dragon' may reach 9 feet), trumpet lilies need adequate but unobtrusive staking. For a more natural look, give each stem its own stout cane rather than tying a group in to a single stake. First-year bulbs may reach only 4 feet, but as they mature, you can expect them to be as much as 6 or 8 feet tall. Decked with pendant blossoms, the stems become very heavy, calling for serious support. A skinny piece of bamboo won't cut it, but rebar stakes work very nicely, as do half-hoops of bent rebar (see Chapter 7, "Practical Pointers").

Though all trumpets are beautiful, none are lovelier than the 'Moonlight' strain, which runs from pale chartreuse through glimmering gold. The possible exception is 'Midnight', a muted, magical night shade that appears now red, now purple, now nearly black, depending on the light. Delicious, apricot-colored 'Lady Anne' looks incredible against a backdrop of silvery artemisia or dim purple hazel leaves, as does the bolder, tangerine-and-bronze 'Copper King'. It hardly matters which you choose, since all are extravagantly satisfying plants. What matters more is to plant lilies in large enough groups to make a real impact. This means using a minimum of three to five bulbs per clump, even in small gardens.

Tiger Lily (Lilium tigrinum)

Tiger lilies arrive in high summer, blooming unfazed through the dog days. The old standards are all tawny oranges, their bright faces freckled with brown or wine red spots. Newer varieties come in wonderful tints of butterscotch and cream, raspberry and rose, old gold and buttery yellows, all of them as cheerful and adaptable as their ancestors. Native to China and Japan, the tiger lilies (which include the related species Lilium lancifolium) have been hybridized with numerous others over the years, and many wonderful new lilies owe their fortitude to these sturdy growers.

Like other stem rooters, tigers and their hybrids appreciate good soils with quick drainage and plenty of humus. They bloom in sun or light shade, producing long-lasting, recurved flowers on airy stems from late July into September. Perhaps the most beautiful of the forms is a

Northwestern hybrid called 'Tiger Babies', a vigorous grower that offers up a lengthy succession of broad-petaled blossoms in salmon and peach during high summer, just in time to echo the voluptuous blossoms of the hybrid tea rose 'Just Joey'.

Mexican Tiger Flower *(Tigridia pavonia)*

These really should be called leopard flowers because they are spotted rather than tiger-striped. However they are named, they are charming blossoms that suggest three-winged butterflies. Three small inner petals are heavily speckled, while the three large outer petals, unspotted and flaring at their edges, curve inward at the heart to make little soup bowls full of freckles.

The true species is lacquer red with black and gold spots, but what is usually offered is a mixture of hybrids in sunset colors. Occasionally one finds pure, unspotted flowers in softer colors, and it's worth remembering that any form with special appeal can be lifted and grown apart if you want to preserve it. (Indeed, that's exactly how most named forms are found.)

Like so many summer bulbs, tiger flowers crave sun, space, and an open soil. Where drainage is less than perfect, it is safer to lift the bulbs for the winter. On a hot, sunny bank, they can be given a blanket of mulch and left to colonize freely, multiplying year after year.

Southern Bugle Lily *(Watsonia)*

These cheerful South Africans send up wide ribbons of irislike foliage threaded with short spikes of tubular flowers in late summer. In recent years, a number of hybrid color forms have been available, from both specialty catalogs and general nursery catalogs. One of the best is 'Rubra' (3 feet), with burgundy red, open bells on strong, branching stalks. 'Pink Opal' (to 3 feet) has curving, pearly pink trumpet flowers, while those of 'Mrs. Bullard's White' (2½ feet) are chalky.

Bulb mixtures tend to run to hot reds and oranges, which work wonderfully with bronze-and-copper-leaved coral bells (*Heuchera* spp.) as well as with similarly colored chrysanthemums. For a more cooling effect, try backing them with periwinkle blue *Aster* × *frikartii* 'Mönch' and a richly marbled border barberry, *Berberis thunbergii* 'Rose Glow'.

Watsonias aren't picky about soil quality, but demand perfect drainage and full sun. They love seaside situations or hot city gardens with lots of reflected heat and light from nearby buildings and streets.

Calla Lily (*Zantedeschia aethiopica*)

Calla or arum lilies have exceptionally graceful lines, their single petals overlapping in smooth embrace about sturdy stalks. The thick petals have the texture and color of heavy cream, unrolling in a fascinating manner from long, spearlike buds. Though most people think of them as hothouse cut flowers, several forms are soundly hardy throughout the region. *Zantedeschia aethiopica* 'Crowborough' is a clean, porcelain white chosen by Graham Stuart Thomas for hardiness and good garden habit. Given full sun and rich, moist soil and kept groomed of fading flowers, 'Crowborough' blooms off and on from late June into autumn.

Flower arrangers and artful gardeners are wild about *Z. aethiopica* 'Green Goddess', a creamy calla that is heavily brushed with green. Both have large, tropical-looking leaves like elongated, glossy, bottle green hearts. A deep winter mulch will protect both forms from the harsh arctic fronts that whistle down our way every few years. In mild winters, the plants may not go fully dormant until the new year.

A number of very pretty tender callas are available as well. Flowering in shades of cream, pale orange, yellow, rose, and shell pink, these make lovely pot plants but will need to be carried over indoors for the winter (see Chapter 6, "Bulbs in Containers").

The Bulbs of Autumn

CHAPTER 3

September, October, November

In many gardens, Labor Day signals the end of the growing year. This is a pity, because gardeners who throw in the trowel so early are missing out on all sorts of fun. For one thing, autumn is an ideal time to plant trees and shrubs, divide early bloomers, and transplant summer perennials. In addition, there are so many seasonal pleasures to savor, from shimmering grasses to spangled seed heads, many of them wonderful sources of food for birds, which flock to well-stocked gardens when natural supplies grow short. Last but hardly least, a goodly number of late-blooming plants are just waiting to be discovered and enjoyed.

Although foliage plants that spark and catch fire in fall take center stage, a trugful of lovely bulbs will happily accompany them. Some, like the late-blooming lilies, are summer leftovers, as are many of their perennial companions. Others, like the flaunting, rosy flowers of naked ladies (*Amaryllis belladonna*) and the ribbon-candy curls of Guernsey lily (*Nerine bowdenii*) are true children of the harvest season.

For gardeners who never want the year to end, it's especially rewarding to build dazzling vignettes that celebrate the richness of autumn. Masses of dusky asters make a splendid foil for the ripe red berries of *Iris foetidissima*, while the glossy new leaves and chubby fruiting spikes of Italian arum (*Arum italicum* 'Pictum') glimmer between clumps of wine red *Helleborus* 'Early Purple'. Experiment freely to find your own favorite season extenders, but be prepared to add a lot of plants to the garden as each new one captures your imagination or your heart.

Italian Arum (*Arum italicum* 'Pictum')

This fascinating little European lives backwards compared to most garden plants, making its contributions during the quieter seasons. *Arum italicum* 'Pictum' (8 inches) is related to skunk cabbages and Jack-in-the-pulpit, sharing the familial hooded flower shape. However, this one produces its new foliage in fall, keeping company with hardy cyclamen and autumn crocus (*Colchicum*). The leaves are lovely—tapered, arrow-shaped, and beautifully marbled in cream and sage. Plump, tomato-colored berries, thickly clustered on sturdy, short stalks, persist well into winter in some gardens.

It's easy to overlook the green, slender-hooded flowers that arrive in midspring and linger into summer, but they will look charming nestled between ruffled ferns and glossy barrenworts (*Epimediums*). Italian arums grow happily in sunny situations, but they also tolerate root competition and dry shade. This makes them invaluable in mature, woodsy Northwestern gardens, where they will brighten up the understory from November into May.

Naked Lady (*Amaryllis belladonna*)

Older gardens throughout the region are apt to have a clump or two of these fragrant, silky-pink creatures. Sometimes called "magic lily" for its trick of appearing out of nowhere to decorate the August garden, *Amaryllis belladonna* (to 3 feet) blooms on naked stems, long after its leaves have faded away. The broad, ribbony foliage emerges in early spring and is entirely gone by midsummer, so these big bulbs should be tucked between leafy perennials that will hide the awkward foliar demise without smothering the late-arriving flower stems. Set between silvery artemisias and blue rues or clumping grasses, naked ladies will toot their hot-pink trumpets well into September.

Autumn Crocus (*Colchicum*)

Not a true crocus, *Colchicum autumnale* (6 inches) is a lily cousin that produces its graceful, crocuslike flowers all fall. The hefty corms are so vigorous that if you don't plant them soon enough, they will begin to send up clusters of long-necked flowers while still in their bag (or even while sitting on the kitchen table). Though fun to watch, such precocity is not actually good for the bulbs, which should be planted as soon as you get them, usually during their brief summer dormancy (normally July and August).

The regular species form is a pinky lavender, but named forms like 'The Giant', with large, lavender blossoms, and the double, violet-petaled 'Waterlily' are also available. A close relative, *Colchicum speciosum*

'Album', which sends up great white goblets of bloom, is considered to be the best of the autumn bulbs. A blanket of dead nettle, *Lamium maculatum* 'White Nancy', makes a dramatic setting for this one.

Autumn crocus sends up leafy, smothering cabbages of foliage early in spring, and the bulbs multiply quickly in ordinary garden conditions, so allow each bulb plenty of room (12–18 inches apart is about right). Since the lush leaves are also among the most obtrusive in their death throes, these bulbs require careful placement if they are to grace rather than disgrace the garden. They are best kept to the back of the border, where they can be admired when the remains of summer's display have been tidied away. Tuck them under shrubs with outstanding fall foliage, such as *Fothergilla major* or purple-fruited beautyberry (*Callicarpa bodinieri*), for a delightfully rich effect.

Crocus (*Crocus*)

Quite a few genuine crocus species flower in fall. Though most are collector's rarities, a couple are readily available from nursery catalogs like Wayside and Van Bourgundien. Expensive but quick to multiply, the Greek *Crocus goulimyi* (6 inches) is the choicest, offering beautifully shaped lavender flowers, long-necked and fragrant, in October and November. It likes a well-drained, sunny garden spot, as does *Crocus speciosus* (6 inches), a variable species with numerous named forms. Most are in shades of lavender, lilac, mauve, and pale blue, but there is also a pretty white form, 'Albus'. Both species will grow well in the border, but either can also be grown in grass under open, deciduous trees that lose their leaves early in the autumn.

Hardy Cyclamen (*Cyclamen*)

The shimmering florist's cyclamen that fill the grocery stores in winter have smaller, wildling relatives that bloom out of doors from late summer well into winter. Hardy cyclamen have the same reflexed flowers, unfurling from long, skinny buds into flocks of silken butterflies. Most bloom pink and rose or white, but a few have rich purple throats and markings. Cyclamen leaves are handsome as well, rounded and glossy and often marvelously mottled with pewter or stippled with sage and cream.

Among the easiest to please is the ivyleaf cyclamen, *Cyclamen hederifolium* (8 inches), a Mediterranean with splendidly patterned, deeply lobed leaves and purple-pink flowers. The species is quite variable, and there are some lovely selected forms like 'Pewter Leaf' and 'Silver Leaf' as well as white-flowered 'Album'.

European sowbread, C. *purpurascens* (6 inches), was fed to swine in winter, a shocking waste of its intensely fragrant magenta blossoms and dappled, heart-shaped leaves. In Northwestern gardens, it emerges from dormancy and begins to bloom in high summer and continues in fits and starts through the winter solstice. The foliage remains remarkably handsome well into spring, fading into dormancy by midsummer.

Tolerant of dry, even rooty shade, hardy cyclamen make themselves at home snuggled right up to the trunks of mature trees or skirting border shrubs. They take a year or two to settle in, but soon begin seeding themselves around.

When you plant, allow each plant plenty of room, for a happy cyclamen can double in size each year. (In elderly gardens, you can find cyclamen plants with tubers the size of a garbage-can lid.) The rounded tubers look like inflated Frisbees, and it takes a good eye to discern the top, with its rounded, bumpy growing points, from the bottom, with its wispy bits of clinging old roots. Once you figure it out, plant them shallowly, covering each with no more than an inch of soil. If you are planting late and frost threatens, top them off with loose mulch rather than more soil.

Oriental Lily (*Lilium*)

The group known as Oriental lilies (3–6 feet) come into their own in late summer, and many of them carry on well into autumn. Tall and open in form, these hybrids retain something of the grace of their several parent species (mostly the dazzlingly fragrant *Lilium auratum*, the gold band lily, and the rosy *L. speciosum*). Though a few are upfacing, most carry wide-petaled, drooping blossoms that nod gently on long stalks.

Like most stem-rooting lilies, Orientals prefer rich, moist (but always well-drained) soils and deep mulches. They are always willing workers, and their bloom is especially prolonged when they are grown in light or partial shade. Their height makes them vulnerable to wind damage, especially after hard summer rains, so they benefit from the protection of nearby shrubs and trees. Only the tallest need staking, except in open, exposed situations or dense shade.

'Casa Blanca' is one of the prettiest Orientals, with enormous yet delicately shaped blossoms tumbling off 5-foot stems. They are pure white with a pale green heart, unmarked except that the wide inner petals are daintily embroidered with tiny white French knots (really a kind of floral fringe called *papillae*). The slimmer outer petals curl fatly sideways at the tips to reveal faint lemon-juice markings on their back sides. This one is prodigal with its fragrance, which it sends through the garden in enticing wafts.

A newer variety, 'Kyoto', is quite similar but more compact, and its crisp white petals are dusted with rose pink speckles. Several outstanding strains are variations on this theme, including 'Imperial Gold', with wine-spotted white petals longitudinally striped in clear gold, 'Imperial Silver', with shining white flowers with cinnamon spots and stamens, and 'Imperial Pink', with rose-speckled blossoms the color of raspberry ice cream.

Rubrum Lily

The rubrum lily, *Lilium speciosum* var. *rubrum* (2–4 feet), is a parent of the Oriental lilies, and certainly worth growing in its own right. It's hard to say whether the petals are actually pink or whether they are white but stained with strawberry and speckled with ruby. Each blossom has a glowing green heart edged in white, from which the long, cinnamon-tipped stamens emerge in little bouquets. A more open, rather larger flowered form, 'Uchida', blooms in August and September, on taller (4–5 feet), well-branched stems. A number of exciting new forms are entering the market, including sparkling 'White Angel' and the breathtaking 'Wing Dancer', its glowing baby-pink petals fringed with white, almost hairy-looking markings (papillae) above a narrow green heart.

Autumn Snowflake (*Leucojum autumnale*)

Snowflakes are overgrown cousins of the nodding snowdrops that brighten the new year. Although most snowflake species bloom in spring, *Leucojum autumnale* (6 inches) sends up its slender bloom stalks in September, soon followed by thready foliage. Although only a few of the delicate white bells grace each stem, a few bulbs will quickly build into a sizable colony, making for a better show of bloom.

Snowflakes crave sandy, fast-draining soil, so those who garden on clay will need to add lots of coarse grit to their planting site. Reflected light and heat from walls or landscape rocks will also speed the multiplication of these little bulbs. Indeed, snowflakes need all the light they can get, even when dormant, so be sure their resting place is not shaded or overcrowded during the summer.

Guernsey Lily *(Nerine bowdenii)*

When fall crisps the air and the garden sags in splendid, slumping swags, the vigorous, upright stalks of Guernsey lilies punctuate billows of netted bronze fennel or felted gray sages like little pink explosions. A stalwart South African, *Nerine bowdenii* (18–30 inches), is the hardiest of the family, shaking out its sizzling pink curls from flame-shaped buds in September and October. A tall beauty, 'Pink Triumph', waits until she has no competition (late October or even November), so that her satin-pink flowers may be fully admired. Enticing hybrids like glossy red 'Cherry Ripe' appear in local nurseries from time to time, but they are usually staggeringly expensive and are not lastingly hardy without the protection of a cold frame in winter.

No matter how deeply you plant them, *N. bowdeniis* are always pushing their snouty brown bulbs out of the ground, but it's sensible to set them 4 to 6 inches below the soil surface the first year, when they can use an extra degree of frost protection. Once they reposition themselves to their liking, they will withstand even hard freezes with aplomb, although a loose winter mulch is advisable when arctic blasts threaten.

To get the most from their long-lasting flowers, give these cheerful creatures a sheltered, sunny nook out of the wind and protected from rain. (They love to grow against south-facing walls.) Ordinary soil is fine unless it is extremely tight clay, which should be improved with plenty of grit and compost before planting.

Rain Lily *(Zephyranthes candida)*

Awakened by the return of the autumn rains, *Zephyranthes candida* (12 inches) is a reliable late bloomer for sunny Northwestern gardens. In summer, its grassy little clumps of foliage look unprepossessing, but with the rains come soft, small flowers like flattened crocuses. These are enchanting little goblets, their inner petals tinted with pink and lacquered as buttercups, the outer petals snowy.

They are undemanding plants, wanting only a place in the sun and excellent drainage. Snug them between stones on an exposed path or an open terrace, poke them into the crevices of a rock wall, or scatter them in small clusters between evergreen Mediterranean herbs like rosemary and sage on a sunny bank.

The Bulbs of Winter

CHAPTER 4

December, January, February

In most places, the winter months are a time of waiting. The garden is fallow and the gardener is tucked up by the fireside, poring over catalogs and illustrated books, dreaming of the spring to come. Here in the Northwest, the picture can be quite different. Nobody can really have June in January, but anybody who cares to try can have something in bloom or berry on any day of the year. Winter iris often begin to bloom in November, continuing to send up silky, fragrant blossoms until March. The marbled leaves of *Arum italicum* 'Pictum' remain lovely all winter. Hardy ferns and hellebores become beautiful backdrops for snowdrops and daffodils, crocus and scilla, that flower in January and February. When we add some or all of the willing creatures mentioned below to our gardens, the dead of winter is brought to life.

Grecian Windflower (*Anemone blanda*)

Innocent as daisies, Grecian windflowers (*Anemone blanda*, 6 inches) arrive with the warming chinook winds to herald the end of winter. Delicate in appearance, they are ruggedly robust in constitution, blooming freely in all sorts of sites and situations. During late winter, their tightly furled foliage emerges from the frosty ground in knuckled knobs, glazed and purple with cold. By March, they are blooming with abandon, which they often continue to do for several months without respite.

Children of the sun, windflowers hold their fringed blossoms tightly closed during inclement weather, which helps keep them looking fresh over their extended blooming period. As soon as the sun comes out, they expand into a blanket of bloom, completely hiding their frizzy, parsleylike foliage.

Most nurseries carry windflowers in color mixtures that include white, soft or rosy pinks, and various shades of blue. To find the following selected color forms, you will probably have to turn to a specialty catalog (see the appendix "Regional Resources"). It's worth a bit of trouble to seek them out, for single-color strains are essential ingredients in concocting some of spring's most memorable plant partnerships.

Large-flowered 'White Splendor' is a classic that combines readily with almost anything, from lemony daffodils to baby blue forget-me-nots or fire-engine red tulips. Gentle 'Pink Star' has delicate pink rays and a cool white throat, a pleasantly pastel plant that complements the pink-and-blue bells of the silver-spotted lungwort, *Pulmonaria saccharata* 'Mrs. Moon'.

The very expensive new windflower selection *A. blanda* 'Radar' is a rather harsh hot pink, closer to magenta than the rose it is generally called. This one needs strongly toned companions like *Bergenia cordifolia* 'Rotblum', with hot red blossoms and glossy, leathery leaves. Though its tints do vary somewhat, *A. b.* 'Blue Shades' is a reliable and lovely seed strain with a high percentage of lavender blue flowers. These set off whites and yellows nicely, but also add snap to deep-toned 'Purple Parrot' and 'Blue Aimable' tulips.

PLEASING WINDFLOWERS: Windflowers do well in windy, exposed places, tolerating even dry, poorish soils, but they bloom best and longest in good garden soil with adequate moisture in winter and spring. Where summers are actually hot (they claim this happens in Oregon), windflowers settle in sooner and multiply faster in light or partial shade than in full sun. Big colonies are easily divided by chunking up bits with your trowel as soon as the flowers have faded. Set these starter clumps here and there about the borders, and in a few years they will form thick drifts of spring stars.

When you open a packet of windflower tubers, you find hard little pieces of dried protoplasm with no discernible top or bottom. To figure this out, soak them for a couple of hours in tepid water; when they are rehydrated, it's easier to see the bumpy little growth points on the tops and the faint, whiskery rootlets on the bottom. If you still aren't sure which way is up, play it safe and plant them on their sides. The emerging roots will pull the tuber into position all by themselves, and the flowers will emerge a lot sooner if their stems don't have to circumnavigate their own storage units.

Crocus (*Crocus*)

The portly Dutch crocus that flower in spring are the easiest kind to find in nurseries and garden centers, but there are many others that beat these slowpokes into bloom. First off the mark are the species sold collectively as snow crocus, so named for their propensity to open their slender buds in January no matter what the weather. These mixtures are usually excellent buys, consisting of strong growers that flower reliably early. The color range is generally confined to watercolor blues and muted lavenders, with a few creams and orange-yellows thrown in.

If you prefer your crocus in masses of single colors, look for the earliest bloomers by name. Golden bunch, *Crocus ancyrensis* (4 inches), is among the first to open, its soft orange flowers appearing in lax clusters around New Year's in mild years. Another early bird, *C. laevigatus* 'Fontenayi' (6 inches), has warm lavender blossoms with gunmetal stripes on their back sides.

By the end of January, *C. fleischeri* (4 inches) is generally beginning to bloom. Its narrow white petals give it a starry look, aided by a glowing heart full of fluffy golden stamens. This one has a mild, wild scent that is strongest on warm, still days, a sweet reward for gardeners who weed on their knees. *C. tommasinianus* (4 inches), or tommies, as they are fondly known, can be counted on to open their lavender blue blossoms in January unless the winter is truly horrendous.

A variable bunch bloomer, *Crocus chrysanthus* (6 inches) has given rise to scads of named varieties, all of which bloom in February and March. Best known is 'Advance' (4 inches), cloudy purple in the bud, opening into cups of glowing gold. Dainty 'Cream Beauty' (4 inches) is a buttery blond, while buxom 'Blue Bird' (6 inches) opens wide petals that shade from grape to skim-milk blue. Pure white 'Snowbunting' makes a charming companion for 'Prince Claus', with smoky lavender buds and clean white cups.

All are worth planting, so snap up any you find and give them a try. Snow crocus are not picky about soil so long as it is well drained. They will bloom well under deciduous trees and shrubs, or anyplace where they get plenty of light in winter and spring. However, bulbs planted in gravelly, sunny places, between paving stones or near heat-reflective walls, will flower soonest.

Hardy Cyclamen *(Cyclamen coum)*

Quite a few fall- or spring-flowering cyclamen are sporadic winter bloomers, but only one species is thoroughly reliable in this respect. *Cyclamen coum* (6 inches) opens its rosy butterflies from January through March, the slim stalks unwinding in graceful curves that are repeated backwards when the shiny little seeds are ripe. It's fascinating to watch this slow process, for the pods always split just over the parent tuber, dumping the seed in glossy little mounds in midspring. Busy ants soon arrive to carry them off, and you quite often can trace their trail back home by tiny seedling cyclamen that pop up in their wake.

Like most hardy cyclamen, *C. coum* has remarkably pretty foliage as well as those fetching, reflexed flowers. The rounded, heart-shaped leaves are a lustrous, deep green, and though often unmarked, some forms are faintly mottled with silver tracery. Patient gardeners willing to wait a few years for results will learn that seed-grown plants often yield forms with softer pink or white flowers. Those who like rewards right now will be glad to hear that several nurseries sell selected seedlings by color. These look charming next to winter-blooming heathers or nestled closely around variegated *Daphne odora*.

PLEASING HARDY CYCLAMEN: Hardy cyclamen prefer open-textured soils enriched with humus, tolerating moderate drought better than an excess of water. The flat, rounded tubers should be planted when dormant, usually sometime between June and August. They are often partially exposed in natural settings, but in the garden it's wise to plant them an inch or so below the soil surface where they won't dry out.

Though happy to receive full sun in winter and early spring, cyclamen prefer to be well shaded during the warmer months. They will snuggle happily against the trunk of a mature deciduous tree or any similar place where they will be moist in winter but relatively dry in summer.

Winter Aconite *(Eranthis)*

Spangling the grass like glossy golden coins, winter aconites open sometime in February, keeping company with Lenten roses (Oriental hellebores). Looking much like their cousins the buttercups, aconites have similarly lacquered petals centered with fluffy golden stamens. Encircled by fringed ruffs of deeply cut foliage, the single flowers stand on wine-dark stems just a few inches tall.

The most commonly available species is *Eranthis hyemalis* (4 inches), a European woodlander with small, lemony flowers and fine-textured foliage. A terrific Turk, *E. cilicica* (4 inches), offers slightly larger flowers and skinnier leaves, but they are really much of a muchness, so either kind is worth buying.

Better than either parent is a splendid hybrid called 'Guinea Gold', with big, lustrous flowers and coppery new foliage. This is also (wrongly) sold as *E. tubergenii* 'Guinea Gold', so named after the famous Dutch nursery where it was introduced around the turn of the century.

PLEASING WINTER ACONITES: Any decent garden soil will suit winter aconites, and once you get them started, they are easy to grow well in moist, shady spots. They grow beautifully in borders when they receive full sun in winter and spring but are well shaded in summer. They also hold their own nicely in grass, particularly if sited beneath deciduous trees.

When people fail with aconites, it's because the tubers have been allowed to get too dry. Ideally, the rough, lumpish little things should be transplanted "in the green"—a phrase meaning after the flower has faded but while the foliage is still green. Unfortunately, this is possible only if you have friends blessed with lots of seedlings. Tubers bought from catalogs (even good ones) tend to be severely dried out, and a good percentage of them will fail unless they are soaked for a few hours or even overnight in lukewarm water before planting. Try to soak and plant your aconites as soon as they arrive. Never let the packaged tubers sit around in sunny or warm places waiting for you to remember them.

When you do plant, don't worry about orientation; just set them an inch or two deep. The tubers know better than we which way is up, and if planted in late summer will set themselves straight by spring. It can take a couple of years for aconites to settle in, but *E. hyemalis* may begin to seed into colonies in just a few seasons. The others will need periodic division—every five years is about right—just split up overgrown clumps in the green, set small patches about, and let them slowly spread into carpets of gold.

Snowdrop (*Galanthus nivalis*)

In mild winters, snowdrops often appear with the new year. Their tightly sheathed buds curve on slim stalks, their white petals opening at the first hint of thaw. The common snowdrop, *Galanthus nivalis* (6 inches), is a model of graceful simplicity. Grouped in threes, the large, outer petals are clean white and textured like slubbed silk, while the flimsier inner petals are marked on their outsides with green fish or hearts and neatly penciled with green inside.

Despite their apparent delicacy, snowdrops are impressively tough. On a cold morning after a hard frost, the clumps seem melted to mush. A few hours later, the warming sun revives them and they rise again, crisp and fragrant.

In garden settings, snowdrops need no special care other than protection from errant shovels. They bloom equally well in sun or shade, and though they emerge earlier in light, sandy soils, they also thrive in heavy ones. In the border or in grass, snowdrops spread fairly quickly if allowed to ripen seed and foliage fully. To speed the process, split and reset large clusters while the foliage is still green.

Iris reticulata

February sees the first flowers of *Iris reticulata* (6 inches). This rock-garden treasure is small in stature, yet so vivid in color and form that a cluster of a dozen bulbs calls the eye clear across the garden. Most of its named selections are in shades of blue and purple, but ivory 'Natascha' and sea foam–tinted 'Katharine Hodgkin' are notable exceptions.

Clarion yellow *Iris danfordae* is very similar, but this one has a tendency to split into dozens of frail, undersized bulblets after blooming the first year and then disappear. Plant these netted bulbs deeply (4–6 inches below the soil surface) to avoid this problem. (The others prefer to be planted under 2–3 inches of soil.)

Reticulated iris are very long lived if given a sunny spot in well-drained soil. They rot quickly if given too much summer water or if their ground space is overgrown, but will otherwise multiply nicely. Divide established clumps every three or four years and reset the bulblets in clusters of ten or a dozen for the best display.

Daffodil (Narcissus)

Most of the border narcissus flower in spring, but a hardy handful are true flowers of winter. Several species classed as hoop-petticoat daffodils produce their tiny trumpets in February. Those of chalky lemon *Narcissus bulbicodium* (5 inches) have fluttery little corolla petals (really perianth segments) surrounding full, flaring trumpets (coronas), while moonlight-pale N. *cantabricus* (4 inches) has smaller trumpets and threadier petals.

In some gardens, these diminutive creatures prove tough enough to thrive in turf, but they are better off in a protected border spot that can supply the usual bulb requirement for plenty of sun and excellent drainage.

Dapper Spanish N. *cyclamineus* (8 inches) flowers look like little garden squids, for their corollas are so reflexed that they stand straight up above the narrow trumpets. This curious creature has given rise to a flock of pretty hybrids, among them 'February Gold' (12 inches) and softly tinted butter-and-cream 'Dove Wings' (14 inches), which opens in late winter. Sunny yellow 'Tete-à-Tete' (7 inches) offers its cheerful little trumpets in twinned pairs. The blossoms last a very long time, for mine are nearly always in bloom for my youngest son's birthday in mid-January, yet remain in good form into March.

The cyclamineus group is unusual in preferring a lightly shaded spot in relatively moist (but not soggy) soils, where a few bulbs may increase slowly into generous clumps.

Squill (Scilla)

These flowers of spring are frequent winter visitors, and several species can be counted on to appear in force by the end of winter. Siberian squill, *Scilla sibirica* (5 inches), is nearly always awake to keep company with the last of the snowdrops. An energetic Russian, it sends up tufts of grasslike leaves in midwinter, each clump soon spangled with open bells, sometimes single, but more often in open clusters of two or three. These are the color of mountain lakes, each petal striped in summer-sky blue. The effect is an intense blue that stands up nicely to the equally strong rose of *Cyclamen coum*, and the two look very pretty planted together. A selected form, 'Spring Beauty' (4 inches), has paler, lavender blue flowers striped with cobalt, while 'Alba' blooms in clean white, though there are also some delicate white forms marked with watercolor green.

A little less common but just as easy to grow, *Scilla bifolia* (4–6 inches) has starry, upfacing flowers centered with fizzy yellow stamens. This is a variable species with several distinct forms, some tall, dark, and handsome, others diminutive and gently tinted. Most are periwinkle blue, but a few are porcelain pale and at least one is white with a lemon throat and golden stamens. The form sold as S. b. 'Rosea' blooms a bit later than the species, and its shell pink flowers are sometimes less abundant. To encourage this relative weakling to flourish, give it a protected spot without competition.

The squills thrive in ordinary garden soils, but they can rot in heavy, tight clays unless their planting site is amended with grit and humus (compost and aged manure work wonders). Though enjoying winter and spring sunshine, the squills are woodlanders that appreciate light or dappled shade in summer. They look very much at home in woodsy rhododendron gardens or in mixed borders, especially if planted among deciduous shrubs. Not ardent colonizers, squills left undisturbed will nonetheless slowly spread into pools of blue that bridge the gap between winter and spring.

CHAPTER 5

Bulbs in Borders

When we introduce bulbs into permanent garden settings, a number of considerations must be addressed before we set trowel to soil. Unlike potted bulbs, garden bulbs are expected to thrive on their own with relatively little intervention. However, established beds and borders are full of plant neighbors, many of which will compete with bulbs for food and water, air and space. One goal is to develop healthy plant relationships, combining plants with similar cultural needs. There are also aesthetic questions to consider, beginning with the most practical. Which plants have both similar needs and bloom times? Which combinations will be mutually supportive, both visually and in terms of life and dormancy cycles?

Learning the answers to these questions takes a bit of research, but fortunately the work is of the most delightful kind. Browsing through books and catalogs, you can glean a good deal of general information to act as a guide for your initial experiments. Even more valuable is the practice of keeping a garden journal and writing down your observations about the things that are happening in your garden. Over the years, you amass a significant body of specific information that applies directly to your own situation.

In time, creating lovely, effective plantings that mingle bulbs with shrubs and perennials will feel like second nature to you. Fortunately, the learning stages are also full of pleasure and profit, so any efforts you put into developing planting skills are very quickly repaid. Learning how to use bulbs well not only increases their life span but amplifies both the beauty of their display and our enjoyment of it.

COMPANIONS FOR SPRING BULBS

Bright, buxom, and blazingly beautiful, big border tulips and daffodils are often the mainstay of the spring garden. As long as they are planted with a lavish hand, it's not hard for the rankest beginner to create a sumptuous display with these ebullient creatures. It's a bit trickier to use little bulbs like crocus and snowdrops well, but even these small-scale minor bulbs can have surprising impact if they are thoughtfully planted. This is partly a matter of generosity, for few bulbs, big or small, are structural enough to shine when dribbled around the garden in ones and twos. Most, however, look great in groups, which means planting in tens and twenties in small gardens and by the hundred in larger ones.

The way bulbs look is also influenced by the company they keep. Although it can be hard to visualize the garden of spring when you are planting bulbs in autumn, it's important to consider what kinds of neighbors your bulbs will have when they awaken from their long winter's nap. One almost foolproof approach is to plant clusters of bulbs in front of hedges or tucked into the bays between smaller shrubs nestled into the borders. Most flowers appear to best advantage when given a firm supporting backdrop of evergreen shrubs, and bulbs are no exception. Dwarf rhododendrons, andromeda (*Pieris*), and hardy hebes are all fine candidates, as are fragrant daphnes and sweet box (*Sarcococca*).

Since even compact border shrubs are considerably larger than most bulbs, some early-blooming perennials will help make a smooth visual transition between these two elements. Lungworts (*Pulmonarias*) with plain or spotted leaves are terrific bulb companions, blooming abundantly in shady Northwestern gardens. Sweet violets, bright-faced spring pansies, and nodding bluebells are also good candidates. Primroses of all sorts are solid performers in these parts, and many of them will rebloom a bit in autumn as well.

In sunnier gardens, steel blue *Euphorbia myrsinites*, with its long, lax arms covered in soft, overlapping scales, makes a fascinating friend for ornamental onions as well as species tulips. Bowles' golden grass, *Milium effusum* 'Aureum', glitters in lemony, sun-catching strips between yellow and white daffodils. Indeed, many of the smaller ornamental grasses combine fetchingly with bulbs large and small, providing delightful contrasts of texture and form as well as color.

COMPANIONS FOR SUMMER BULBS

Where the spring bulbs were the stars of the garden, summer bulbs are apt to take secondary roles, outshone by their perennial neighbors. A few, like lilies and the larger crocosmias, command considerable attention, but most require thoughtful placement to be fully appreci-ated. This means not only meeting their cultural requirements, but dis-covering lastingly appropriate garden partners for each kind of bulb.

All bulbs—indeed, all plants—are most apt to thrive when both these conditions are met. Tuck rot-prone lilies into well-drained, humus-rich pockets between slow-growing border shrubs, and they will flourish for years to come. Give jaunty tiger flowers a place in the sun with mannerly and upright companions, rather than sprawling ones that shade the bulbs out, and they will reward you with many happy returns.

The smaller summer bulbs in particular, like the blue dicks (*Brodi-aea*) and delicately colored camas, need a proper setting if their charms are to be readily visible. Since brash or outsized companions will readily overshadow these minor bulbs, pair them with understated partners. Set vivid blue *Brodiaea laxa* 'Queen Fabiola' against pleated fans of banana-and-cream variegated iris or the silver lace of mugwort, *Artemisia absinthium* 'Huntington Garden'; place chalk-blue camas against foamy chartreuse lady's mantle (*Alchemilla mollis*); in each case, their most subtle details of coloration and modeling will become delightfully apparent.

Certain summer bulbs are structural enough to perform as focal points in mixed company. Exotic voodoo lilies (*Dracunculus*), Jack-in-the-pulpits, and snowy callas (*Zantedeschia*) all contribute both striking flowers and unusual, dramatic-looking foliage to the garden tapestry. Tall crocosmias like 'Lucifer' and 'Firebird', and certain Siberian iris, have magnificent foliage, upright and luxuriant as any grass. The stiff blades of angels' fishing rods (*Dierama*) arch like living fountains over a wash of vivid 'Blue Ensign' morning glories. All of these boldly built bulbs make potent vertical accents amid a sea of billowy perennials.

To set off the strength of their form, give these powerful perform-ers supportive but secondary partners. Sprays of crocosmia fan out like peacock tails above fuzzy silver carpets of woolly lamb's ears, *Stachys byzantina*, and curving clumps of coppery New Zealand grasses like *Carex buchanani* or *C. flagellifera*. Spurts of Siberian iris foliage flare above mounds of lemon-lime cushion spurge, *Euphorbia polychroma*, and cascades of blue catmint, *Nepeta* 'Six Hills Giant'. The long, taper-ing leaves of voodoo lily contrast excitingly with the huge, cloudy flower heads of sea kale, *Crambe cordifolia*. Great, club-shaped Jack-in-the-pulpit leaves add counterbalance to groups of rounded hostas and netted ferns. Broad calla foliage makes a visually pleasing link between big, shield-shaped hydrangea foliage and the velvety, angel-wing leaves of Jerusalem sage, *Phlomis russeliana*.

It is enormous fun to experiment freely with bulb placement, seeking always to create memorable pictures with the living pigments of our plants. In each case, the plants are paired and positioned to accentuate each other's strengths of form, color, and texture. Naturally, you don't have to re-create the exact combinations mentioned in this book; they are intended simply as guides for the imagination. Hundreds of attractive combinations are possible, and if they don't work out or suit your taste, just try something new. As long as we keep their basic needs in mind, most plants are amazingly forgiving. Indeed, a visitor once remarked that perennials ought to come equipped with wheels to facilitate their frequent travels about the garden. Bulbs are even more adaptable, for if moved when in or approaching dormancy, they won't even notice a change of address.

COMPANIONS FOR AUTUMN BULBS

As summer wanes, the garden is apt to look rather worse for wear. A good grooming session soon after Labor Day refreshes tatty borders, preparing the way for the autumnal beauties yet in store. It's quite fun to sail through the beds, tugging out yellowing stalks and browning leaves here, cutting back empty seed heads and spent blossoms there. Don't get too zealous in this hacking stage, however, or you end up with nothing but stubble. Allow the season its due, for signs of maturity and impending winter are not objectionable in themselves. Only the truly unsightly and the overtly dead must go. Even such gentle grooming will have surprising impact, and you will find the garden a far pleasanter place to spend time when it is not full of silent reproach.

Because they are invisible for much of the year, fall bulbs need especially thoughtful placement. The trick is to find them spots that will permit them to shine undimmed while the garden about them is dimming, and will also allow for their needs all through the year. Although most are dormant during the summer, fall bloomers need the same respect for their turf as any other bulbs. Since large gaps are rarely welcome at the front of our summer borders, it makes sense to group fall-flowering bulbs toward the middle and back of the beds. Tuck white

Colchicum speciosum 'Album' under compact evergreen rhododendrons, surrounding them with the silvery dead nettle *Lamium maculatum* 'White Nancy'. Nestle hot-pink *Amaryllis belladonna* beneath the skirts of deciduous shrubs with great fall leaf color, like *Fothergilla major* or *Spiraea japonica* 'Goldflame'. This gives them both a context, without which bulbs look lonely and misplaced, and a backdrop to frame their flowers effectively.

It also helps to choose places where the front parts of the border are reduced to foliar tapestry. This way, bulbs placed deeper into the beds are not obscured by lots of late bloomers. It makes perfect sense to use such late bloomers in combination with the bulbs and shrubs, but they should be flanking or backing up the lower-growing groups. Tall asters and Japanese anemones, fluffy goldenrods, and fizzy purple *Verbena bonariensis* are all terrific candidates for fall bulb vignettes. (Vignettes are extended combinations that often include plants of many kinds—bulbs, shrubs, perennials, and so on.)

COMPANIONS FOR WINTER BULBS

By winter, most of the garden is put to bed. Slumbering roses are heaped with rotted manure, while the resting crowns of perennials are tucked up to their chins with thick blankets of mulch. What remains is the structure of the garden, what is often referred to as "garden bones." Artificial constructs like paths and patios, columns and trelliswork give the garden its winter shape, which may be further defined by fences or walls. Structure can also come from plants, whether evergreen hedges or shapely trees. Small clusters of compact, evergreen border shrubs provide islands of texture and tone amid the beds and borders, and make splendid settings for the bulbs of winter.

Such clusters need not be large to be effective. Indeed, in a tiny garden, a single rhododendron could comfortably shelter five or six kinds of winter bulbs. Clumps of snowdrops and crocus bloom companionably from midwinter on, while the rosy, upswept flowers of *Cyclamen coum* appear in fits and starts all winter long. Golden winter aconites (*Eranthis hyemalis*) join the throng as spring draws near, as do the tiny yellow trumpets of *Narcissus* 'February Gold'.

To round out the picture, add a few evergreen perennials, perhaps the early-blooming *Helleborus* 'Early Purple' (also called *H. atrorubens*) or some clumps of midwinter-flowering *H. orientalis*, with roselike flowers in pink and cream. Glossy green barrenworts such as *Epimedium grandiflorum* or the lustrous *E. perralderianum* keep their fresh good looks all winter, although their flowers don't appear until early spring. Evergreen ferns, airy and netted, make beautiful bulb backers as well, including crested male ferns like *Dryopteris filix-mas* 'Cristata' or 'The King'.

SUCCESS WITH BORDER BULBS

It's important to remember that no matter when they bloom, all hardy bulbs need to rest and ripen without being crushed beneath the lush growth of their perennial neighbors. Choose open areas of the border for your bulb plantings, and allow plenty of space for expansion. When we are tucking tiny bulbs between the small resting rosettes of our perennials in early spring or late fall, it's easy to forget that both bulbs and perennials will be far larger come June, and larger still each succeeding year. It can be very helpful to scratch a circle around each perennial to indicate its mature size before placing your bulbs. Ideally, when both bulbs and perennials are in full fig, they will overlap enough so that you won't see bare earth between them, yet the bulbs will not be smothered by exuberant foliage.

Hardy bulbs will last longest and increase most readily when allowed all the room and time they need to complete their full life cycle, from shoot to fading foliage. Resist the impulse to tidy away browning bulb leaves, for they must ripen naturally in order to store their summery energy back into the bulbs themselves. It is fine to tuck obtrusively yellowing leaves underneath those of companion plants. Indeed, it is always a good idea to choose plant partners that can perform this kindly screening function as the bulbs wither. Compact border shrubs and large, leafy perennials do this nicely, and so long as every plant has enough room to grow well, competition problems rarely arise.

CHAPTER 6

Bulbs in Containers

As we browse through bulb catalogs, our eyes are often caught by glowing pictures of exotic bulbs like gloriosa lilies (*Gloriosa rothschildiana*), with their flaming fingers of red and gold, or curly-petaled Peruvian narcissus (*Ismene*). When we see them listed as "hardy to zone 9," we may simply shrug our shoulders and dismiss them as too tender to be worth trying in this climate. However, these tender beauties and many others can be coaxed into bloom if potted up and encouraged to sprout indoors. Once well established, they may be moved outside, pot and all, to enjoy the warmer months on the deck or in the border. Although they won't survive many (if any) winters out of doors, when sheltered in a frost-free garage or sunporch for the colder months, many tender bulbs will flourish in their pots for years.

Then too, quite a few tender bulbs make splendid houseplants when properly treated. Most valuable of these are off-season bloomers like the South African amaryllis that appear everywhere (even in grocery stores) as the winter holidays draw near. Although most people toss them away once their glorious trumpets have faded, properly treated amaryllis can be both long-lived and astonishingly beautiful, producing flower stems by the dozen as they become mature.

There is also a great deal of pleasure to be gained by forcing precocious bloom from plants that would be perfectly hardy in the garden. Hyacinths and freesias, crocus and narcissus are all excellent candidates for the cold treatment required to coerce winter flowers from spring-blooming bulbs.

POTTING BASICS

Many garden texts make much of the need for scrupulous care in potting bulbs. Indeed, by the time you finish reading the complicated instructions for sterilizing pots and soils, you begin to feel as if your very touch might be contaminating. After a few messy and frustrating attempts to fulfill those stringent requirements, I noticed that plants left in their pots from year to year, even when moved from indoors to outdoors, seemed to do fine without any remedial sterilization. At that point, I began to pot indoor bulbs exactly as I do outdoor ones, and the results have been unequivocally successful.

These days, I scrub pots only if they are heavily stained with mineral salts from excess fertilizer. Otherwise, I simply tip the old soil into the compost heap, then refill the containers with fresh compost. If you don't have a compost heap, use a balanced potting mixture like Whitney Farms' Uncle Malcolm's Special Blend. (No, I don't own stock in the company—but they are a family-owned regional resource that supplies consistently high-quality products.)

When planting up really large pots and containers, begin by putting several inches of grit or gravel at the bottom to promote quick drainage and good air flow to the plant roots. With really huge containers, you can fill the bottom third with those ubiquitous plastic packing peanuts. They work as well as grit in terms of drainage and significantly lighten the final weight, making it much easier for a smaller person to move or reposition oversized pots without help.

When planting bulbs in deeper pots and containers, I often layer in several kinds and sizes, making a sort of floral sandwich. Bigger bulbs like tulips or giant fritillaries go in first and are covered with an inch or two of soil. Next come midsized things like hyacinths or checker lilies, which are topped with another inch of soil. Last to be positioned are tiny bulbs like crocus, anemones, and species tulips. These receive a final inch or two of soil, and then the whole is topped off with an inch of fine-textured mulch.

Once filled, pots and containers should be watered from the bottom when possible. Usually, this is done by setting filled pots into pans of water so that the liquid is absorbed through the base of the pot. This reduces soil shifting, which can lay bare our bulbs, exposing tender roots to harsh light and more air than they really appreciate. Oversized containers must be watered from above, but adding a watering rose attachment to your watering can or hose will minimize soil disturbance. (A watering rose is not a flower, but a sprinkler head with tiny perforations that produce an even and gentle flow of water that imitates soft rain.)

FORCING BULBS

It's enormous fun to fill the house with flowering bulbs in winter. The huge Israeli paperwhites called 'Ziva', extravaganzas of white and gold, smell almost overpoweringly sweet indoors, while the smaller, citric yellow 'Soleil d'Or' have a spicier fragrance. Plump, queenly amaryllis open regal trumpets on the breakfast table, some royal crimson, others icy green and white or candy-striped in pink and cream. A few hours spent preparing the way in late September or early October will provide us with pots of flowering snowdrops, plump purple crocus, or sky blue squills by mid-December.

If you want to extend the picture, you can pot up a few perennial companions as well. Sweet violets (*Viola odora*) and wide-eyed primroses (*Primula vulgaris*) that are potted up in autumn and chilled in a cold frame can be brought indoors when the forced bulbs begin to sprout. Given a warm, sunny spot inside, these perennials, too, will blossom early to brighten table or windowsill along with your bulbs.

Reefer Madness

In order to persuade bulbs to blossom early indoors, we need to give them an extended period of cold treatment. Here in the Pacific Northwest, autumn and early winter may be as mild as late summer, so simply potting bulbs up and leaving them outside in a cold frame won't get the job done, as it does in colder climates. Instead, we must resort to refrigeration.

There are two ways to go about chilling bulbs, both of them good. Traditionalists insist that bulbs should not go naked into that chilly if artificial night. These people always pot up their bulbs first, and then subject them to cold treatment, pot and all. To do this, plant your bulbs in their pots, cover them with soil, then water well, allowing excess water to drain away. Before chilling, cover each pot with a plastic bag to conserve moisture, closing it loosely with a twist tie. Then set the pots in the reefer and wait.

Now, some families have been known to object when the refrigerator is suddenly fuller of pots than of food. Bulb pots do take up quite a bit of space, and some of us have found it politic to invest in an inexpensive secondhand fridge for such activities. This may seem indulgent, yet mine comes in surprisingly handy all year long. Perhaps there is a terrific sale on something perishable, or the summer garden harvest arrives in a rush. Indeed, during holidays when lots of entertaining is going on, it can be hard to find room in there for my bulb pots, thanks to the press of party food.

If you can't spare the space for an extra fridge, just slip your bulbs (still in their mesh or paper bags) into tightly closable plastic bags, including plenty of air. These can be tucked discreetly into the vegetable bin or behind the mustard, often without arousing unfavorable comment. Since they don't have the protection of soil during their long weeks of chilling, check the chilling bulbs periodically. Make sure they are neither too damp (which may cause molds to grow) or too dry (this makes them shrivel up like old onions or potatoes).

If the bulbs do look damp, take them out, wipe them dry, and repack them with a few teaspoons of dry milk powder in each package. This will absorb any excess moisture from the bag without desiccating the bulbs themselves. Should the bulbs look too dry, repack them in a tighter sealing bag, adding a bare sprinkle of water first. Check up on them again in a few days, repacking in a dry bag if they now seem to be too moist.

These precautions may seem bothersome, but in fact, they are rarely necessary. Still, it's worth taking the time to check up on your investment rather than losing the lot to the creeping blue crud that lurks in many an outwardly respectable refrigerator. When the bulbs' dormancy time is up, pot them up in the usual way and set them aside to root and sprout.

Coming in from the Cold

Where you sprout the bulbs depends on how you keep your house in winter. Most people's comfort zone is too warm for plants, even bulbs that think spring is just around the corner. An unheated sun porch is an ideal place to sprout forced bulbs. Often the basement or garage will be cooler than the house yet warmer than the out-of-doors. In an elderly, drafty house like mine, no place is really too warm for bulbs. I often set mine under the kitchen table, below the sunny windowsill where they will eventually bloom.

Wherever they end up, the forcing pots should be kept moist but not soggy. As soon as the first shoots appear, move the pots into a warmer, sunnier spot. Turn the pots each day so that the shoots grow evenly rather than stretching toward the light. Forced bulbs usually have lankier foliage than those grown outside, so some solid support is welcome. Skinny bamboo skewers (the short kind sold for kebabs) are perfect for this job. Use at least three sticks for each pot, and wind a discreet web of black thread or clear fishing line around and between them. Held by these netted threads, the foliage will remain straight and tidy.

Forcing Table

Bulbs should be chilled at temperatures above freezing (32°F), but below 40°F. The longer times indicated are for bulbs chilled in relatively warmer refrigerators.

Bulb	Weeks of Cold Treatment
Windflowers (*Anemone blanda*)	8–10
Crocuses (*Crocus* species)	8–10
Checker lilies (*Fritillaria meleagris*)	10–12
Hyacinths (*Hyacinthus*)	12–15
Reticulated irises (*Iris danfordae*)	10–14
Reticulated irises (*Iris reticulata*)	10–14
Snowdrops (*Galanthus* species)	9–12
Grape hyacinths (*Muscari* species)	10–14
Daffodils (*Narcissus* species and hybrids)	12–15
Squills (most *Scilla* species)	10–12
Tulips (*Tulipa* species and hybrids)	12–16

TENDER BULBS

Many tender bulbs can be planted right in the ground in combination with shrubs and perennials. Grown this way, gladiolas, dahlias, and begonias can be treated as annuals and left to die with the first frosts. This rough-and-ready method has the appeal of great simplicity, and it's an excellent way to sample all sorts of wonderful plants without creating an unwieldy collection. However, few of us can so readily abandon the more expensive and less common tender bulbs. These can be lifted in late autumn, as described below, and carried over the winter in storage. Tender bulbs can also be grown in permanent pots or containers, making winter storage much simpler.

Autumn Care for Tender Bulbs

Those glorious gladiolas and bright begonias will heartily enjoy summer in the garden, but if we want to preserve them for another season, they will need to be gathered in before hard frosts arrive. In late autumn, when killing frost is rumored, dig the favored plants up carefully. In thickly planted gardens, use a small border fork or a narrow poacher's shovel to avoid chopping into their neighbors' roots or skewering too many of the bulbs you are trying to save (you nearly always stab a few, but this is simply part of the process and no cause for guilt).

Next, shake the roots free of soil. This is easy enough when the ground is dry, but in wetter conditions you may need to let the plants dry out for a day or two. Set damp bulbs in a dry place, out of direct light, placing each kind on its own sheet of paper. It's very helpful to write the name on each sheet as soon as you do this, because you will not, in fact, remember which each is tomorrow, let alone next week, however plain this information seems at the time.

Potted plants that you want to reuse in a different manner next year can be dumped out onto a sheet of newspaper for sorting. If a pot contains only one kind or contains several very different kinds, this is a simple task requiring little concentration. If, however, very similar looking bulbs are planted in layers, remove the dirt with your hands and unpack each kind of bulb separately to keep them straight. Again, give each its own sheet and label them as you go to avoid confusion.

Once the bulbs are dry, remove any excess dirt and trim off all foliage and top growth. Give them another few days on newspaper in a dry, cool place, always out of direct light, to complete the curing process. This may take time, especially in a soggy year, but adequate curing (the drying and conditioning of bulbs) makes all the difference to the success of the process.

While you wait, you can make labels for each type of bulb. The extra-long white plastic plant labels allow plenty of room to record details like color and size while you still remember them. These labels will later be attached to the bulbs' storage bags and containers.

Winter Storage for Tender Bulbs

Once clean and well cured, the bulbs can be packed loosely in paper or mesh bags (the kind vegetables come in). Place the label inside each bag, and then store the bags where they will remain dry and get plenty of air but little light. The rafters of the attic or basement are great spots, as are any places that would do for drying herbs or flowers.

In older houses or sheds where mice are plentiful, you can keep bulbs safe by hanging them on long loops of string with a foil pie plate between the rafter and the bag. Punch a hole in the center of the pie plate (a big nail works well) and thread it on the string, using a few knots to keep it in position. The airy, screened boxes used for drying fruit are also excellent places to store bulbs. Closed boxes can also work, but only if they allow plenty of air exchange (to avoid rots) while protecting the bulbs from furry pests.

Winter Storage for Bulbs in Containers

Bulbs in more or less permanent pots and containers will almost always need to be brought in from the cold, even when the bulbs are quite hardy. Many pots, especially those made of clay, are highly susceptible to frost damage, and borderline-hardy bulbs that would winter over unscathed in the ground may get too cold for comfort in a container. Exceptions include those huge concrete planters that are all but immovable in any case; most hold enough soil that hardy bulbs (and other plants) can thrive in them for years.

Traditional places to store pots for the winter include an unheated basement, garage, or shed. They also do well in a cold frame or an unheated greenhouse, tucked to rest beneath the benches. During the coldest months, all they really need is a dry, airy place that provides shelter from severe cold (neither pot nor bulbs should actually freeze). While the pots should never dry out completely, their soil should be kept barely moist until late winter, when the bulbs' roots begin rapid and active growth.

Winter Protection for Tender Bulbs in the Garden

In garden settings, the best way to protect half-hardy or borderline-hardy bulbs is to give them a thick blanket of mulch in late autumn—6–8 inches is not too much. You can also invest in plastic or glass coverings called cloches, each of which protects a single plant or cluster of bulbs. Cloches can be lovely (and pricey) antiques or plastic milk jugs with their bottoms cut off; both work equally well.

Garden umbrellas also provide effective protection from frost and from excess rain, which is an important factor in carrying certain heat lovers through our wet Northwestern winters. These are made of transparent, heavy-gauge plastic, with a stout, pointed stake instead of a curving handle. They can be set in place over larger colonies of tender or very recently planted bulbs (which should still be well mulched). They stand up amazingly well to wind and even snow, but unfortunately are attractive to cats, who love to bask under them, soaking up the warmth (and squashing the plants). A small handful of naphtha-based mothballs or moth flakes makes a convincing deterrent.

CHOOSING TENDER BULBS

This very partial listing of tender bulbs gives a glimpse of the richness in store for adventurous gardeners. Some, like amaryllis, are familiar plants that can be far more rewarding if treated with patience and understanding. Others are less common but equally easy to please. Success with these may well entice you into long and happy relationships with a host of exotic tender bulbs that can brighten your home and garden all year round.

Amaryllis (Hippeastrum)

Amaryllis need not bloom and die; if watered and well fed through the year, they develop into splendid mother bulbs, gaining in girth and dignity as they mature. Each fifth leaf produces a bud stalk, so the more leaves you can coax from the bulbs, the greater the flower display. If given a large enough pot, these big bulbs soon begin to produce bulblets, which cluster at the mother bulb's side. These can be removed and grown on, but if left in place, they build into spectacular groups. Provide large, shallow bulb bowls for amaryllis bulbs, using a gritty, open soil with quick drainage.

To keep them growing well, keep amaryllis moist but not sodden as long as they exhibit active growth. Feed them twice a month, using a combination of liquid feeds for a good balance of trace elements. Allow blossom stalks to ripen before removing them (but do cut away any seed heads, which will drain away reserve energy from the bulbs). Trim off browning leaves as they fade.

In summer, amaryllis appreciate a place in the sun, indoors or out. Keep them moist and growing strongly all summer. In September, bring the plants back inside. Give them a sunny spot, but cut back on water—allow the soil to become fully dry between waterings—and stop feeding the bulbs. Around Thanksgiving, begin regular watering again. As soon as new growth appears, resume feeding the bulbs. By the solstice holidays, you should be enjoying brilliant blooms again.

Begonia (*Begonia*)

Frilled like petticoats or ruffled as rosebuds, tuberous begonias are long-blooming bulbs that can be wintered over and reawakened each spring for many years. They rarely grow well in the ground, where their lush foliage is delectable to slugs and very susceptible to rot when overgrown by larger companions. However, begonias are stellar performers in hanging baskets and window boxes. The plump tubers should be sprouted indoors in flats or pots, planted in a rich but well-drained potting mixture. Keep them moist and allow them plenty of indirect light, and soon fat little shoots will appear. As soon as their leaves unfold, increase their water and begin weekly feedings, using half-strength liquid fertilizers. By the time they can safely be taken out of doors (usually late April or early May), these hard workers will be in full leaf and covered with buds.

Begonias bloom well in light or dappled shade, but need plenty of light (if not direct sunlight) to be continuously productive. Full sun may be too much for them; any that look scorched or dry should be moved to half shade. Being heavy bloomers, they demand copious amounts of water and may need daily watering in hot weather. Since so much water flushes away nutrients, feed them every other time you water, using various fertilizers at half the recommended strength.

Basket Beauties

Basket begonias make handsome plants, up to 1 foot high and 2 feet across, their glossy, bronzed foliage curving like wings, each leaf flushed with burgundy underneath. Single flowers look like single roses, with five wide petals encircling a spangle of golden stamens. The doubles may have frilled petals or look like fat rosebuds the size of a teacup. They bloom in a delicious palette, including rose and salmon, peach and raspberry, and ranging from yellows and buffs to ivory and clean white.

Non-Stop begonias (8–10 inches) are compact, remarkably floriferous versions of the big doubles, and if kept fed and watered, they really do bloom all out all summer. The flowers are smaller but exceptionally profuse, in a full range of colors from red to white through pinks, oranges, and yellows. The outsized Picotee begonias have big petals neatly deckled with a contrasting color, rose on cream or tangerine on apricot. Carnation begonias (fimbriatas) have a finely cut or laciniated edge to their petals, so they look as fringed as carnations.

Cascade begonias are splendid pot plants with a lax habit, rising to 1 foot but tumbling in streams of blossom to as much as 3 feet when happy. The big, wing-shaped leaves are lovely, often a rich, matte forest green with wine-stained edges. The flower stems are also dark red, throwing clusters of buds on long, dangling stems. They produce both single and double flowers, rose or white, pink or yellow, or many shades in between. The Cascade Flamingo begonias have fancy, frilly flowers ruffled as a dancer's skirts, in soft, sherbety shades that are all mutually compatible.

Dahlia (*Dahlia*)

The buxom, oversized dinner-plate dahlias are the best known, but few plants are more difficult to grow well. Each blossom needs staking (and sometimes its own umbrella as well), and they tend to overshadow all neighbors. However, dahlias come in many sizes and types, from diminutive window-box dahlias to the bouncy decoratives, which make the best all-round garden plants. Decoratives (to 3 feet) have hand-sized flowers with tiered, tightly packed petals that may be as dark as midnight red 'Arabian Night' or as pale as 'Eveline', whose cream blossoms are delicately edged in lavender lace.

Smaller border decoratives (to 15 inches) have correspondingly smaller flowers, but are exceptionally floriferous over a long period if well fed and frequently deadheaded. These bloom in rich reds and purples, as well as buff and biscuit and citrusy yellows and oranges. The Redskin series boasts ruddy leaves (some nearly black) and coppery red or orange flowers that look dramatic against purple or wine red foliage plants. Long-blooming anemone dahlias have a large central boss and fewer but broader petals. These do very well in containers, as do tiny window-box dahlias (10–15 inches), pretty little daisy-flowered singles that are practically everblooming when well groomed and well fed.

Spiky cactus dahlias look like sea urchins, while the wildly swirling spider dahlias are reminiscent of spiky chrysanthemums. My personal favorites are the Mignon patio dahlias (20 inches), big singles with broad overlapping petals that give them the look of more substantive annual cosmos.

Gladiola (*Gladiolus*)

To get the most from gladiolas, give them rich, gritty soil in full sun. Plant them deep (6–8 inches), and rotate their position in the beds each year to avoid pests and problems. Plant in dozens or more for impact; several groups of the same color will make pleasing repeats in border or bed. Their tall sheaves of swordlike foliage make terrific balancers for the cloudy, billowing mounds of less shapely perennials. Hybrid gladiolas come in a fascinating array of colors, including green and smoky gray, tans and tawny buffs, or the exact shade of coffee with cream. These are always sought after by colorists seeking to develop artful effects.

Peruvian Daffodil (*Ismene festalis*)

Peruvian daffodils (*Ismene festalis*, 12–15 inches) are tender amaryllis cousins with similarly strappy, glossy leaves. Frilly as orchids, the tubular white flowers are surrounded by twirling, thready petals that give them the look of little fireworks. They need rich but gritty, open soil and all the sun we can muster in this part of the world. In sheltered gardens, they may survive for years in the ground, but most of us are better off planting these charmers in pots and bringing them indoors during the coldest months. Plant the bulbs shallowly, a mere inch or two below the soil surface, and feed them generously from the time their shoots emerge until the foliage begins to brown off. Dry them out slowly in autumn to prepare them for winter dormancy, but leave the bulbs in their pots and keep them barely moist, for the fleshy roots should never dry out completely.

Tuberoses (*Polyanthes tuberosa*)

Tuberoses are exceptionally fragrant relatives of the century plant (*Agave*), as their spiky fans of foliage proclaim. Native to Mexico, they hate Northwestern winters with a passion, but can be persuaded to rejoin us summer after summer if well treated. Give them deep pots with open, sandy soil, using three or four tubers in each 8-inch pot. Keep them consistently moist but never sodden and provide plenty of food, and you will be rewarded with spire after spire of those intensely perfumed white blossoms. Let them dry off gradually in fall, but never let the roots become completely dessicated. Tuberoses must winter over indoors, for even a few degrees of frost will prove fatal.

Calla Lily (*Zantedeschia*)

Tender hybrid calla lilies are smaller than their hardy cousins, seldom exceeding 15 inches. All are creamy in color and lovely in shape, with the smooth familial spathe wrapped around narrow spadix. Their big, crinkled leaves are deckled with little spots that prove on closer inspection to be translucencies, like tiny windows in the leaf. A number of wonderful forms are available from both nurseries and catalogs, sometimes by color, otherwise in mixtures. A softly lemony one is unpoetically called 'Yellow', joined by chalky 'Pink' and 'White', the latter actually a buttery, moonlight yellow. Mixtures include mellow shades of pink and rose, pale cream, ivory, and banana- or yolk-yellow forms. Give them deep pots, gritty but humus-rich soil, and constant moisture (but never let them drown). They bloom well in partial shade, but often scorch when given too much direct light.

Practical Pointers

Although the maritime Northwest is prime bulb-growing country, it is still important to understand the needs of our bulbs if we are to grow them well. It's hard to generalize about bulbs' cultural requirements, since some bulbs grow happily in shady swamps while others can survive only in pure gravel and full sun. However, the bulk of border bulbs are adaptable creatures that have proven themselves garden worthy in many places and over many years—in some cases, centuries.

Part of what makes bulbs so popular is their dependability. When we buy daffodils and tulips from reputable growers, we are buying blossoms that have already been formed. Each bulb contains the incipient leaf and flower, tucked safely inside this natural storage container. To fail with well-grown bulbs, you really have to resort to abuse. It isn't impossible; leave unopened bulb packages in the hot sun for a month or two, soak them in rainwater, let them mold in the basement—we all know a trick or two for circumventing nature. But give those daffodils or tulips a chance—plant the bulbs as soon as you buy them, in decent soil and a reasonably sunny site—and their flowers are virtually guaranteed.

To understand the cultural needs of less familiar bulbs, we need to know where they came from. Woodlanders such as avalanche lilies and hardy cyclamen prefer light or dappled shade and loose, fluffy soils with lots of humus. They do best in spots that are damp in winter and spring yet dry in summer. Species tulips and bulbous iris that hail from open plains and steppes prefer deep, loamy, well-drained soils and plenty of sunshine. They too want to be moist in winter and spring, but they like their summers both dry and outright hot. Mountain dwellers such as certain daffodils and crocus prefer lean soils with excellent drainage, and may also require dry winter conditions, something that can be tricky to manage in these parts.

MAKING BEAUTIFUL DIRT

There are a few general rules about pleasing bulbs in Northwestern gardens. Like any plant, a bulb's most basic needs are soil and water, light and air. First in importance is decent soil. Nearly always, providing good garden soil will be enough. Ideally, of course, this means that elusive dream: loamy, humus-rich soil that holds just enough moisture to please thirsty roots yet drains excess water away quickly. If you are gardening on such soil, you are fortunate indeed. Plant anything you like and buy a hammock, for the results are likely to be almost effortlessly splendid. If, however, you live in the real world with the rest of us, read on.

Pleasing Bulbs in Clay Soils

Many of our native Northwestern soils are heavy, clay-based, and uncompromisingly acid. Although they support an astonishing variety of native flora, once stripped of their natural plants they may prove surprisingly infertile. The blue clays in particular need significant amendment before they can be considered good garden soils.

The first thing to add to clay soils is humus. This can (and should) come from a wide variety of sources. Use as many kinds of humus as you can muster, for each brings its own supplements of trace elements and minerals. While needed only in tiny amounts, these act like plant vitamins and enable plants to make the most of the nutrients you supply. Some of the most common humus additives are compost, aged manures, shredded bark, chopped leaves, and rotted straw.

Compost is perhaps the most useful, since it typically has dozens of ingredients. Grass clippings, border gleanings, autumn leaves, and kitchen scraps are turned through garden alchemy from trash into black gold, the best soil conditioner around. Certain weeds, notably nettles, chickweed, and horsetails, are splendid compost additions; all are deep rooters that bring significant nutrients to the heap. (Just be sure to add them before they begin to set seed.) The green parts of garden weeds such as comfrey and mints also qualify—but keep those pernicious root systems out of the compost!

Sweetening Acid Soils

Compost is also a good buffer for acid soils. Aged compost made from a range of materials is nearly always neutral, or close to neutral, which means 7.0 on the pH scale. This is especially desirable when garden soils are strongly acid, which means anything under 6.0. If you aren't sure how acid your soil is, invest in a little testing kit. Most nurseries carry these, which are both inexpensive and easy to use. Unless your soil has been gardened organically for a long time, or treated with lime recently, it is likely to prove well under 6.0. While many native plants (as well as non-native rhododendrons and azaleas) like it that way, the majority of garden plants prefer more neutral soil conditions.

We can create less acid soils by adding generous amounts of organic materials to our beds each year, but the process takes time. To speed things up, we can add some lime, which will sweeten our gardens right away. The kind we want is called dolomite or agricultural lime (not hydrated lime, which is intended for outhouses and construction purposes).

Lime is most effective when well mixed into the soil, not just sprinkled on top. This is easiest to do before a bed is planted; add 5 lbs. of lime per100 square feet of soil, then till or dig it in thoroughly to a depth of at least 1 foot. If your garden is already established, this wholesale approach simply isn't practical. In such cases, scatter twice as much lime around the beds, then mix it as well as you can into the top few inches of soil. It makes sense to do this in late winter or early spring, before you replenish weed-suppressing mulches. Dolomite lime lasts for about five or six years, which gives us plenty of time to build healthier soils with frequent additions of compost and organic mulch.

Breathing Room for Bulbs

The next most important soil amendment is coarse grit or what is sometimes called builder's sand. Again, it's important to choose the right kind; mix sandbox sand into clay and you have adobe, an admirable substance if you want to build a house, but less good if you want to plant a garden. Sharper, grittier sand opens heavy soils, allowing air to reach our plants' roots. Roots need to breathe every bit as much as leaves, and when heavy soils lock up, plants can literally smother for lack of air to their roots.

Grit also improves drainage, which can be quite poor in heavy soils. Although most bulbs like plenty of water when they are in active growth, many are susceptible to rots if kept too wet, particularly during dormancy. When bulbs dwindle or fail quickly in heavy soils, planting

Top left: Given a sunny place in the garden, starry *Tulipa turkestanica* flowers from March into May. **Top right:** Chubby bells of spring-blooming checker lily, *Fritillaria meleagris*, are marvelously flecked with heathery colors. **Right:** Graceful, arching avalanche lily, *Erythronium* 'Pagoda', thrives in shady Northwestern gardens. **Below:** The double, lesser celandine, *Ranunculus ficaria* 'Flore Pleno', multiplies quickly in sun or shade.

Top: Spring-blooming Pacific Coast (or P.C.) iris are complex hybrids of native species, all of them lovely. **Right:** Silken blossoms of *Schizostylus coccinea* 'Oregon Sunrise' may appear from November into March in mild years. **Below:** *Crocosmia* 'Firebird' is a vigorous, late summer bloomer that can exceed six feet in height when happy.

Top left: Desert candle, *Eremurus bungei*, flames from mid- to late summer, given plenty of sun. **Top right:** The spherical seedheads of *Allium* 'Purple Sensation' remain sculptural in form even as their color fades. **Bottom left:** Creamy calla lilies, *Zantedeschia aethoepica*, are elegant in form, bold in foliage. **Bottom right:** Both flower and foliage of voodoo lily, *Dranculus vulgaris*, are huge, complex, and showy.

Top left: Glittering globes of
summer onion, *Allium christophii*,
appreciate a hot, sunny spot in
the garden. **Top right:** This
Siberian iris 'Summer Skies',
has sturdy, handsome foliage
that turns golden in fall.
Above: The plump autumn
berries of *Iris foetidissima* may
be tomato-red, orange, yellow,
or white. **Right:** Autumn crocus,
Colchicum speciosum 'Album',
snuggles into a carpet of *Lamium*
'White Nancy' in October.

them in pure grit can work wonders. Dig extra-deep planting holes, then line the bottom few inches with compost and aged manure. This will feed the roots once they are established. Next, add several inches of grit, then place the bulbs on this dry pad. Top them with more grit, and both good drainage and adequate air flow are assured.

It's also vital to remember that bulbs need to breathe even when dormant; if their ground space is taken over by lush foliage in summer, even strong growers may dwindle and die away in just a few years. Place bulbs that crave dry summers under deciduous shrubs or trees, or find spots where excess summer watering won't prevent them from getting their beauty sleep. Just like us, bulbs need to be warm and dry when they nap.

Pleasing Bulbs in Sandy Soils

Light, sandy soils drain almost immediately, but they are often too lean for big border tulips and daffodils. One solution is to concentrate on species bulbs that like poor soils, but even most of these will put on a better show if sandy soils are generously amended with humus. In sunny situations, humus gets burned out of light soils incredibly fast, so adding compost and other amendments becomes an ongoing chore.

When you are preparing new beds in sandy gardens, humus-rich materials can be heaped on as thickly as possible—a foot deep is not too much—before tilling or digging. In established beds, you can add soil-feeding mulches of compost, aged manure, and so forth twice a year; generally this is done in late winter, then repeated in autumn. Generously layer the amendments right on the soil and let the worms do the mixing for you. Take care not to smother the crowns of resting perennials, but don't worry about covering bulbs too deeply; this is almost never a problem.

Mulching Bulbs

Ordinary mulches can also be useful on bulb plantings. In late winter, we can add (or freshen) a layer of finely shredded bark or similar material over early bloomers to keep them clean of splashed mud when those hard spring rains return. Deeper mulches (3–6 inches) help keep gardens free of weeds and unwanted seedlings (again, though, take care not to smother the crowns of dormant perennials). Mulches also keep soil surfaces warmer in winter and cooler in summer, and can significantly conserve soil moisture during the hotter months. Bulbs that like it hot should be mulched less abundantly than those which prefer cool, damp, woodland conditions.

Planting Techniques

When I plant tulips, I always think of my young sons, then aged perhaps four and two, kneeling along the edge of their own little garden with bags of bulbs. As I watched, they took turns shoving tulips into soil tilled not with shovels but with Tonka trucks. As the younger child took his turn, the older said gently, "Now remember, pointy side up this time." When spring arrived, there were a few gaps in the straggly line of tulips, but even those stragglers showed up eventually, having had a longer journey to reach the light and air.

With bulbs that do have obvious tops, pointy side up is indeed a good rule of thumb. Another is to plant bulbs about twice as deep as they are high; that means a 2-inch-tall tulip bulb should be covered with at least 4 inches of soil, while a tiny crocus would be set a mere inch or 2 below the surface. In practice, it is often wise to plant rather deeper than this; bulbs get a bit more frost protection and are less likely to be washed bare by heavy rain or unearthed by hygienically scratching cats or foraging dogs.

Very large bulbs, such as crown imperials (*Fritillaria imperialis*), can be lost to collar rots in this rainy climate, particularly in heavy soils. To reduce the chance of this, add a heaping handful of grit to each planting hole, then tip the bulbs slightly on their sides rather than planting them straight up. The stems will arrive upright and on schedule, but excess water won't be able to collect in the open holes left by the fading stems.

Care and Feeding

Carefree and spectacular as they are in their first year, even sturdy bulbs often produce smaller blooms in later performances and may eventually be reduced to a few leaves and no flowers. This diminishing is the only way a bulb has of asking for food. While few are gross feeders, and some actually prefer lean soils, most bulbs benefit from a feeding mulch in late autumn, with a booster before bloom time (when the foliage is about 4 inches tall). The autumn feed delivers nutrients to the roots that are forming all winter, while the spring or summer booster gives the bulbs something to store up for next year.

Commercial bulb food can be helpful, but less expensive home-made mixtures also work well. Aged manure, compost, and seed meal (cotton or soy) can be blended in equal parts and scratched into the soil above established plantings. Top the area with mulch, and let the rain and worms carry the goodness down to the roots. A generous handful can also be worked into the planting holes of any new additions to the garden.

Staking Tall Bulbs

The tallest-stemmed bulbs, such as trumpet lilies, need adequate but unobtrusive staking. For a more natural look, give each stem its own stout cane rather than tying a group in to a single stake. Rebar stakes work very nicely, as do half-hoops of bent rebar. (Bend the rods with a pipe wrench, using a 50-gallon drum as a shape guide.) Rebar has the advantage of being inexpensive and readily available, and it quickly rusts to an attractive brownish red that blends into the garden far better than the improbable greens of most staking materials.

Proper Grooming

Perhaps the single most important factor in long-term success with bulbs is allowing their foliage to ripen off naturally. This means those browning leaves must not be cut back, braided, fastened off into twists with rubber bands, or any of the other usual tricks gardeners employ to minimize the ugliness. While bulb ripening can indeed be unsightly, it is best dealt with through thoughtful placement. If we provide perennial companions that will screen the passing of our bulbs, they can ripen off in peace without disturbing the beauty of their successors. Just remember to leave enough room between groups, so that as bulbs begin to fade, they can be masked by their neighbors without being smothered.

Pest and Problem Prevention

Here in the maritime Northwest, slugs and, increasingly, snails are perhaps the worst threat to our bulbs' blossoms. After losing hundreds of flowers to hungry gastropods, I have finally resigned myself to the fact that slug bait is a necessity if I want to see a whole narcissus. I don't like to use poisons in the garden, but in judicious amounts, mindfully applied, a relatively less toxic bait such as Corry's can make the difference between outrage and pleasure. Non-toxic diatomaceous earth is an excellent, if expensive, protection as well. As soon as you notice the buds breaking through the soil, encircle them with a small amount of bait. You may need to renew the bait weekly during a wet year.

OF MOTHBALLS AND MICE, MESH AND MOLES: Mice adore all sorts of bulbs, and they like to make their winter nests near a good supply. Gardeners who have found handfuls of peanuts where they planted crocus know that mice are not the only ones to relish bulbs. Squirrels, too, enjoy them, and they probably feel that these interesting little trades alter the nature of their raids from stealing to mere commerce. To convince them otherwise, scatter some of those smelly, naphtha-based mothballs or moth flakes where you have recently planted bulbs. (For some reason, rodents rarely go for established bulbs.)

Moles are sometimes, but not always, put off if you mix some moth flakes into the planting soil below ground level. To foil these marauders, make baskets of ¼-inch mesh hardware cloth and plant your bulbs in these, set at the proper level below ground. Fill them with dirt, arrange your bulbs, then cover them with a flat piece of mesh. Larger bulbs like border tulips and daffodils can be treated similarly, but should be given basket lids of ½-inch mesh to allow room for their fatter stems to poke through.

Appendixes

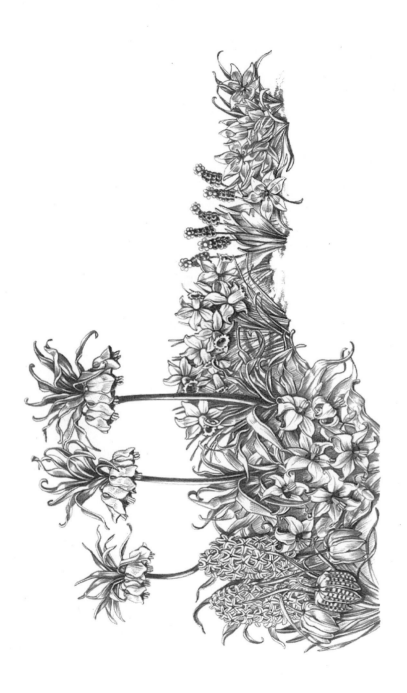

A Spring Bulb Garden

1. Checker lily, Fritillaria meleagris *(10 inches)*; midspring
2. Hyacinth 'Blue Jacket' *(10 inches)*; early spring
3. Fritillaria imperialis 'Lutea' *(3 feet)*; midspring
4. Narcissus 'March Silver' *(12 inches)*; early spring
5. Grape hyacinth, Muscari latifolium *(4–6 inches)*; early spring
6. Tulipa tarda *(8 inches)*; early spring
7. Avalanche lily, Erythronium 'Pagoda' *(12 inches)*; midspring

So many effortless plants bloom in spring, it's easy to assemble colorful garden corners that will be full of flowers from March through May. However, abundance can lead quickly to cheerful chaos unless we are selective in our choices. To paint living pictures instead of producing the usual uncontrolled riot of color, choose a color theme. In this spring garden, the dominant colors are yellow, blue, and white, framed by shades of green, the ultimate garden neutral. Using the same bulb families, we could easily alter this palette to richer runs of reds, purples, and blues, or to cool pastels of pink and lavender and cream.

The same perennial companions can provide a similar range of colors, but a host of others might be included as well. Barrenworts, like the icy white Epimedium × youngianum 'Niveum', add sparkle to delicately tinted bulbs. Bowles' golden grass, Milium effusum 'Aureum', makes sunny threads between bright daffodils and yellow species primroses (Primula veris). Primroses in crayon colors can encircle poppy anemones. Blue-eyed Mary, Omphalodes verna, weaves in running mats under tall pink tulips and rosy-belled hellebores. Shrubby companions abound as well. Give preference to compact border forms, which offer exceptional support to early-blooming bulbs.

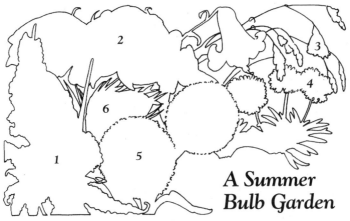

1. *Voodoo lily,* Dracunculus vulgaris *(to 36 inches); midsummer*
2. *Trumpet lily 'Lady Anne' (4 feet), 'Copper King' (6 feet); mid- to late summer*
3. *Angels' fishing rod,* Dierama pulcherrimum *(to 7 feet); early to mid-summer*
4. *Agapanthus × 'Head-bourne Hybrid' strain (to 2½ feet); mid- to late summer*
5. *Allium christophii (to 3 feet); midsummer*
6. *Gladiolus papilio (to 4 feet); late summer*

A Summer Bulb Garden

This little garden will be full during June, July, and August, providing a continual progression of flowers. The color scheme is on the hot side, with lots of ember reds and oranges, though these are gentled by apricot and softer yellows as well as cool lavenders and murky purples. The perennial companions are all foliage plants in soothing blues and silvers, which both set off and temper the stronger hues. There are, of course, many other herbs and grasses that could be used in this role. If you want to use more kinds of plants to make a more interestingly textured tapestry, you can expand the palette to include those other garden neutrals like corn and straw, tan and buff, bronze and copper.

The modest selection pictured here can be extended almost endlessly by adding long-blooming perennials. For instance, one could easily arrange a summer-long succession of blue bellflowers (*Campanula* spp.) and hardy geraniums to accompany the bulbs. Hardy lobelias in shades of purple and blue would also bloom from mid- to late summer; or, if we wanted to intensify the heat of our scheme, we could use some of the dazzling red-flowered lobelias with black leaves and stems.

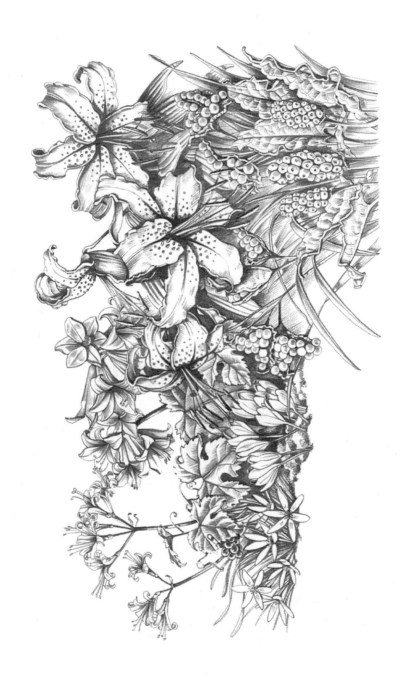

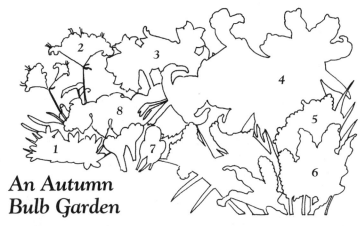

An Autumn Bulb Garden

Ideally, an autumn garden can face southeast, catching the light both morning and evening. This late in the year, all daylight is slanting and soft, but early and late, it haloes the garden in a delicate aureole, gilding everything it touches. In the morning, the strong lines and architectural shapes are softened by golden haze. Flaming fall foliage burns all the hotter when backlit by afternoon sun. The bulbs of fall and their perennial companions look illuminated from within when embraced by the clear gold of autumn light.

For the most part, the bulbs of autumn are modest in form and color, but there are a few exceptions. Bouncing naked ladies

1. *Rain lily,* Zephyranthes candida; *mid- to late fall*
2. *Guernsey lily,* Nerine bowdenii; *mid- to late fall*
3. *Naked lady,* Amaryllis belladonna; *early fall*
4. *Rubrum lily,* Lilium speciosum *var.* rubrum; *early fall*
5. *Gladwin iris,* Iris foetidissima; *fall to winter*
6. *Italian arum,* Arum italicum 'Pictum'; *fall to winter*
7. *Autumn crocus,* Colchicum speciosum 'Album'; *early to mid fall*
8. *Purple grape vine,* Vitis vinifera 'Purpurea'

(*Amaryllis belladonna*) and fizzy Guernsey lilies (*Nerine bowdenii*) flower in singing pinks that glimmer above the glowing embers of the surrounding foliage. Late lilies, white and rose, perfume the air with their heavy, romantic scent. The garden floor is starred with crocus and colchicum, while the sunny pathway is spangled with pink-and-cream cups of rain lilies.

To extend this charming vignette, add plenty of late asters in murky, thundercloud colors, along with armloads of shaggy chrysanthemums in bronze and coppery reds. Silvery sages and wormwoods (*Artemisia* spp.) will add ashy undertones, as will blue-leaved foliage plants.

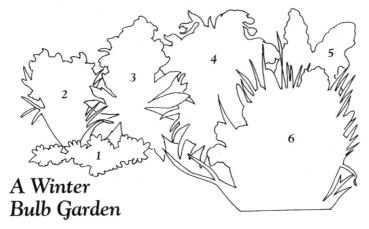

A Winter Bulb Garden

In order to catch the most midday and afternoon light while avoiding morning light (which can cause frozen buds to thaw too abruptly), winter gardens should face southwest. If they can be sheltered on at least two sides by house walls or evergreen shrubs, your winter-blooming bulbs will benefit greatly. For one thing, they will be protected from wind, rain, and snow (rare though that is). For another, either walls or dark leaves will reflect a good deal of warmth and light back to the winter garden area, making a cozy microclimate for your bulbs.

1. **Winter aconite,** Eranthis hyemalis *(4 inches); midwinter*
2. **Daffodil,** Narcissus 'February Gold' *(14 inches); late winter*
3. **Christmas rose,** Helleborus niger
4. **Winter rose,** Helleborus foetidus
5. **Italian arum,** Arum italicum 'Pictum' *(8 inches); all winter*
6. **Iris unguicularis** *(12 inches); autumn and winter*

To make it comfortable for yourself, add a seat or bench so you can take tea in the garden during those astonishingly warm January days that are such an endearing part of the Northwest weather pattern. The first winter iris usually open in early December if the year is mild. Even in a hard year, there will be a bloom or two on *Iris unguicularis* 'Walter Butt' by the winter solstice. These are followed quickly by snowdrops and snow crocus, the eager little species that bloom even through snow. By February, the whole garden is carpeted with a green haze as fuzzy new shoots sprout up everywhere. Next thing you know, golden aconites are spangling the grass and fragrant blue reticulated iris are being relished by slugs. It's time to pay close attention; the year has turned and spring is just around the corner.

Regional Resources

Gardens to Visit

Few public gardens specifically feature bulb plantings except in spring, when bedding-out schemes of bulbs and annuals dominate parks and gardens alike. However, the following places have plantings in which hardy bulbs of various kinds are intermingled with shrubs and perennials. Many bulbs will be blooming in other seasons as well as spring, so you might want to visit more than once. For more ideas on where to find public gardens, consult *Garden Touring in the Pacific Northwest*, by Jan Whitner, and *Visiting Eden; The Public Gardens of Northern California*, by Joan Taylor (see "Further Reading").

BRITISH COLUMBIA

UNIVERSITY OF BRITISH COLUMBIA BOTANIC GARDEN: 6804 SW Marine Drive, Vancouver, BC, Canada V6T 1Z4; (604) 822-3928. *Gardens open daily all year. Free October 9–March 15; seasonal fee.*

VANDUSEN BOTANICAL GARDEN: 5251 Oak Street, Vancouver, BC, Canada V6M 4H1; (604) 266-7194. *Garden open daily all year except Christmas. Fee.*

CALIFORNIA

DAFFODIL HILL: 18310 Ram's Horn Grade, Volcano, CA 95689; (209) 296-7048. *Gardens open daily mid-March–mid-April; closed in rainy weather. Donations appreciated.*

FILOLI: Canada Road, Woodside, CA 94062; (415) 364-2880. *Garden open daily mid-February–mid-November; times vary, so call for specifics. Fee.*

STRYBING ARBORETUM AND BOTANIC GARDENS: Golden Gate Park, Ninth Avenue at Lincoln Way, San Francisco, CA 94122; (415) 661-1316. *Gardens open daily all year. Free.*

SUNSET GARDENS: 80 Willow Road, Menlo Park, CA 94025; (415) 321-3600. *Gardens open weekdays all year. Free.*

WESTERN HILLS NURSERY: 16250 Coleman Valley Road, Occidental, CA 95465; (707) 874-3731. *Gardens open April–October, Wednesday–Sunday. Free.*

OREGON

ELK ROCK: The Garden of the Bishop's Close, 11800 SW Military Lane, Portland, OR 97219; (503) 636-5613. *Garden open daily. Free.*

CECIL AND MOLLY SMITH RHODODENDRON GARDEN: 5065 Ray Bell Road, St. Paul, OR 97137. *Garden open the first Saturday in March and the first and third Saturdays in April and May. Free. To visit at other times, contact the Portland Chapter of the American Rhododendron Society: P.O. Box 86424, Portland, OR 97286-0424; (503) 771-8386.*

WASHINGTON

BELLEVUE BOTANIC GARDEN: The Northwest Perennial Alliance Borders, 12001 Main Street, Bellevue, WA 98008. *Garden open daily all year. Free.*

CARL ENGLISH BOTANICAL GARDENS: Hiram Chittenden Locks (Ballard Locks), 3015 NW 54th Street, Seattle, WA 98107; (206) 783-7059. *Gardens open daily all year. Free.*

LA CONNER FLATS DISPLAY GARDEN: 1598 Best Road, Mount Vernon, WA 98273; (206) 466-3190. *Garden open daily, March–October. Free.*

POINT DEFIANCE PARK: 5402 N Shirley Avenue, Tacoma, WA 98407; (206) 591-5328. *Park open daily all year. Free.*

Nursery Gardens

Nearly all family-run bulb nurseries have gardens or growing fields to tour, as do many other specialty plant nurseries. Because these are often really small businesses, your tour guide is likely to be the nursery owner. You will notice that many owners ask visitors to call first even if the garden is open every day. This is not only courteous, but a real necessity; as every mom knows, it's very hard to stay organized when one is performing a complex job while being constantly interrupted.

It's also important to be a polite visitor. If you take an hour of the owner's time, it's mannerly to buy something at the nursery before you leave. When touring nursery gardens, the same rules apply as when we visit private gardens. Don't pick flowers or leaves or ripe seed heads without asking permission. Keep your feet on the paths or the lawn—even if you have a camera glued to your nose. Don't let pets (or children) run free in the garden. Don't assume you can use the house bathroom.

Though these simple requests seem like common courtesy, they are not so commonly observed as one would hope. When nursery folk seem less than excited to have company, it's probably because the last visitors were less than thoughtful and considerate. All this said, most nursery owners are in business because they love plants and plant people. Most of them are happy to talk plants with like-minded people, time permitting. If you have any doubts about whether a visit is in order, just call ahead to find out.

The following list is limited to regional mail order nurseries. For a truly comprehensive overview of specialty mail order nurseries, get yourself a copy of Barbara Barton's amazing masterwork, *Gardening by Mail* (see "Further Reading"). Updated every other year, this magnificent book lists virtually every catalog nursery in North America as well as a good many overseas. Since Barbara is a librarian, her book is exceptionally well organized and indexed.

Not all of the following are exclusively bulb catalogs, but all offer at least a few uncommon bulbs. Many of these nurseries are also terrific sources for companion perennials, shrubs, vines, and whatnot. Though all are mail order nurseries, many can be visited as noted.

BRITISH COLUMBIA

FERNCLIFF GARDENS (DAHLIAS, GLADIOLAS, IRIS): 8394 McTaggart Street, Mission, BC, Canada V2V 6S6; (604) 826-2447. *Catalog free, $20 minimum order. Nursery open April–September, Monday–Saturday; also October–March, Monday–Friday. Display garden open May–September, Monday–Saturday.*

LINDEL LILIES: 5510 239th Street, Langley, BC, Canada V3A 7N6; (604) 534-4729. *Catalog free. Nursery open June–October, Sunday–Friday; call ahead. Display garden open June–August, Sunday–Friday; call ahead.*

MILLAR MOUNTAIN IRIS NURSERY: 5086 McLay Road, RR 3, Duncan, BC, Canada V9L 2X1; (604) 748-0487. *Catalog $2, $15 minimum order. Display garden open May–June by appointment only.*

MONASHEE PERENNIALS (ALSO IRIS, LILIES): Site 6, Box 9, RR 7, Vernon, BC, Canada V1T 7Z3; (604) 542-2592. *Catalog $2.*

RAINFOREST NURSERY: 13139 224th Street, RR 2, Maple Ridge, BC, Canada V2X 7E7; (604) 467-4218. *Catalog $2, $20 minimum order. Nursery open March–October, Saturdays only; call ahead. Display garden open June–August, Saturdays only; call ahead.*

CALIFORNIA

BIO-QUEST INTERNATIONAL: P.O. Box 5752, Santa Barbara, CA 93150-5752; (805) 969-4072. *Catalog $2, $10 minimum order. Nursery open daily all year, by appointment only.*

BLUEBIRD HAVEN IRIS GARDEN: 6940 Fairplay Road, Somerset, CA 95684; (209) 245-5017. *Catalog $1, $10 minumum order. Nursery open April–May, July–September, Tuesday–Saturday. Display garden open April–May, Tuesday–Saturday.*

CANYON CREEK NURSERY: 3527 Dry Creek Road, Oroville, CA 95965. *Catalog $2. Nursery open all year, Monday–Saturday.*

MISTY HILLS FARMS MOONSHINE IRIS GARDENS: 5080 W Soda Rock Lane, Healdsburg, CA 95448; (707) 433-8408. *Catalog free, $10 minimum order. Nursery open April–May, Saturdays and Sundays only.*

MOSTLY NATIVES NURSERY: P.O. Box 258, 27235 Highway 1, Tomales, CA 94971; (707) 878-2009. *Catalog $3, minimum order $21. Nursery open all year, Tuesday–Saturday. Display garden open April–October, Tuesday–Saturday.*

ROBINETT BULB FARM (NATIVE BULB SPECIES): P.O. Box 1306, Sebastopol, CA 95473-1306; (707) 829-2729. *Catalog free, $10 minimum order.*

NANCY WILSON SPECIES AND MINIATURE NARCISSUS: 6525 Briceland-Thorn Road, Garberville, CA 95440; (707) 923-2407. *Catalog $1, $10 minimum order.*

OREGON

CAPRICE FARM NURSERY: 15425 SW Pleasant Hill Road, Sherwood, OR 97140; (503) 625-7241. *Catalog $2, $10 minimum order. Nursery* *open all year, Monday–Saturday; call ahead. Display garden open May–September; call ahead.*

CASCADE BULB & SEED: 2333 Crooked Finger Road, Scotts Mills, OR 97375. *Catalog: send business-size SASE.*

COOLEY'S GARDENS: P.O. Box 126, 11553 Silverton Road NE, Silverton, OR 97381; (503) 873-5463. *Catalog $4, $15 minimum order. Nursery open all year, Monday–Friday (daily in bloomtime). Display garden open daily in May; call ahead.*

FORESTFARM: 990 Tetherow Road, Williams, OR 97544; (503) 846-7269. *Catalog $3. Nursery open daily all year; call ahead.*

FREY'S DAHLIAS: 12054 Brick Road, Turner, OR 97392; (503) 743-3910. *Catalog $1, $10 minimum order. Nursery open March–October, Monday–Saturday; call ahead. Display garden open August–October, call ahead.*

GARDEN VALLEY DAHLIAS: 406 Lower Garden Valley Road, Roseburg, OR 97470; (503) 673-8521. *Catalog free (send one first-class stamp with request). Nursery open daily August–October. Display garden open August–October; call ahead.*

RUSSELL GRAHAM: 4030 Eagle Crest Road NW, Salem, OR 97304; (503) 362-1135. *Catalog $2 for 3 years or free with order. Nursery open Saturday by appointment only. Display garden open Saturday, by appointment only.*

IRIS COUNTRY: 6219 Topaz Street NE, Brooks, OR 97305; (503) 393-4739 evenings. *Catalog $1.50, $10 minimum order. Nursery open by appointment only. Display garden open May–October, by appointment only.*

GRANT MITSCH NOVELTY DAFFODILS: P.O. Box 218, Hubbard, OR 97032; (503) 651-2742 (evenings). *Catalog free, $10 minimum order.*

OREGON TRAIL DAFFODILS: 41905 SE Louden Road, Corbett, OR 97019; (503) 695-5513. *Catalog free, $5 minimum order. Nursery open all year; call ahead. Display garden open in April; call ahead.*

SCHREINER'S GARDENS: 3625 Quinaby Road NE, Salem, OR 97303; (503) 393-3232 or 1-800-525-2367. *Catalog $4, $10 minimum order. Display garden open daily in late May.*

SHACKLETON'S DAHLIAS: 30535 Division Drive, Troutdale, OR 97060; (503) 663-7057. *Catalog free (send one first-class stamp with request). Nursery open daily August–mid-October; call ahead. Display garden open daily in September; call ahead.*

SWAN ISLAND DAHLIAS: P.O. Box 700, 995 NW 22nd Avenue, Canby, OR 97013-0700; (503) 266-7711. *Catalog $3, $15 minimum order. Nursery open all year, Monday–Friday. Display garden open daily August–September.*

WASHINGTON

AITKEN'S SALMON CREEK GARDEN: 608 NW 119th Street, Vancouver, WA 98685; (206) 573-4472. *Catalog $2, $15 minimum. Nursery open daily April–October. Display garden open daily April–June.*

B & D LILIES: 330 P Street, Port Townsend, WA 98368; (206) 385-1738. *Catalog $3. Nursery open daily July–August; call ahead. Display garden open daily July–August; call ahead.*

COLLECTOR'S NURSERY: 16804 NE 102nd Avenue, Battle Ground, WA 98604; (206) 574-3832. *Catalog $2. Nursery open all year; call ahead. Display garden open all year; call ahead.*

CONNELL'S DAHLIAS: 10216 40th Avenue E, Tacoma, WA 98446; (206) 531-0292. *Catalog $2. Nursery open daily all year; call ahead. (Nursery address: 10616 Waller Road E). Display garden open daily August–September.*

CRICKLEWOOD NURSERY: 11907 Nevers Road, Snohomish, WA 98290; (206) 568-2829. *Catalog $1. Nursery open April–May, Friday and Saturday. Display garden open May–June, Friday and Saturday.*

DAN'S DAHLIAS: 1087 South Bank Road, Oakville, WA 98568; (206) 482-2607. *Catalog $2, $10 minimum order. Nursery open daily August–September; call ahead. Display garden open daily August–September; call ahead.*

DUNFORD FARMS (agapanthus, alstroemeria, hardy cyclamen): P.O. Box 238, Sumner, WA 98390. *Catalog $1.*

LAMB NURSERIES: Route 1, Box 460-B, Long Beach, WA 98631; (206) 642-4856. *Catalog $1.50. Nursery open all year Monday–Saturday. Display garden open all year Monday–Saturday.*

ROBYN'S NEST NURSERY: 7802 NE 63rd Street, Vancouver, WA 98662; (206) 256-7399. *Catalog $2. Nursery open April–June and September, Thursday–Saturday. Display garden open May–September; call ahead.*

SEA-TAC DAHLIA GARDENS: 20020 Des Moines Memorial Drive, Seattle, WA 98198; (206) 824-3846. *Catalog free (send SASE), $10 minimum. Nursery open daily March–October. Display garden open daily August–September.*

SKYLINE NURSERY: 4772 Sequim-Dungeness Way, Sequim, WA 98382. *Catalog $2, $20 minimum. Nursery open all year Tuesday–Saturday. Display garden open June–October, Tuesday–Saturday.*

Other Good Sources for Bulbs

Although the Pacific Northwest is blessed with an abundance of specialty nurseries, we can't always find everything we want right in our own back yard. When certain longed-for plants just can't be obtained locally, it's good to have other options to pursue. All of the following are reputable, reliable sources for special bulbs.

CARROLL GARDENS: P.O. Box 310, 444 E. Main Street, Westminster, MD 21158; (410) 848-5422 or 1-800-638-6334. *Catalog $2.*

THE DAFFODIL MART: Route 3, Box 794, Gloucester, VA 23061; (804) 693-3966. *Catalog free, $15 minimum order.*

PETER DE JAGER BULB CO.: P.O. Box 2010, 188 Asbury Street, South Hamilton, MA 01982; (508) 468-4707. *Catalog free, $10 minimum order.*

DUTCH GARDENS: P.O. Box 200, Adelphia, New Jersey 07710; (908) 780-2713. *Catalog free.*

MCCLURE & ZIMMERMAN: P.O. Box 368, 108 W. Winnebago, Friesland, WI 53935; (414) 326-4220. *Catalog free.*

PARK SEED COMPANY: P.O. Box 46, Highway 254 N., Greenwood, SC 26948-0046; (803) 223-7333. *Catalog free.*

JOHN SCHEEPERS, INC.: P.O. Box 700, Bantam, CT 06750; (203) 567-0838. *Catalog free.*

VAN BOURGUNDIEN BROS.: P.O. Box 1000, 245 Farmingdale Road, Babylon, NY 11702; (516) 669-3500. *Catalog free.*

VAN ENGELEN, INC.: 313 Maple Street, Litchfield, CT 06759; (916) 422-4782. *Catalog free, $25 minimum order.*

WAYSIDE GARDENS: P.O. Box 1, Hodges, SC 28752-0001; 1-800-845-1124. *Catalog $1.*

Further Reading

There are dozens of books on growing bulbs of all sorts, and a few minutes' browse at the local library will probably turn up a goodly list of useful ones. Here are some of the very best for advancing gardeners, fast favorites all. The newer ones will be easy to find, but the older books might take some seeking out. Since there are few more pleasant occupations than passing an idle hour in a good secondhand bookstore, the research is not exactly arduous.

Barton, Barbara, GARDENING BY MAIL. New York: Houghton Mifflin, 1993.

Genders, Roy. BULBS: A COMPLETE HANDBOOK. New York: Bobbs-Merrill, 1973.

Lawrence, Elizabeth. THE LITTLE BULBS. Durham, N.C.: Duke University Press, 1986 (reprint).

Mathew, Brian, and Philip Swindells. THE COMPLETE BOOK OF BULBS. New York: Reader's Digest, 1994.

Phillips, Roger, and Martyn Rix. THE RANDOM HOUSE BOOK OF BULBS. New York: Random House, 1989.

Proctor, Rob. THE INDOOR POTTED BULB. New York: Simon & Schuster, 1993.

THE OUTDOOR POTTED BULB. New York: Simon & Schuster, 1993.

Rix, Martyn. GROWING BULBS. Portland, Oregon: Timber Press, 1983.

Taylor, Joan Chatfield. VISITING EDEN: THE PUBLIC GARDENS OF NORTHERN CALIFORNIA. San Francisco: Chronicle Books, 1993.

Whitner, Jan Kowalczewski. GARDEN TOURING IN THE PACIFIC NORTHWEST. Seattle: Alaska Northwest Books, 1993.

Wilder, Louise Beebe. ADVENTURES WITH HARDY BULBS. New York: Macmillan, 1990 (reprint).

Monthly Chore Checklist

The bulb gardener's year begins not in spring but in fall, when the new bulbs arrive on our doorsteps. Planting bulbs is a lovely way to celebrate the slowing down of the year, for it reminds us that we, like our plants, need to experience the whole cycle of seasons. Gardeners who mourn summer's passing often find consolation in planning and preparing for the spring to come. What's more, when we add autumn- and winter-blooming bulbs to our gardens, those seasons feel less fallow and more full of promise themselves. Instead of only looking ahead to a new spring and the ripeness of summer, we begin to treasure the subtle pleasures of the quieter months.

September–October

Plant new bulbs. Feed established bulb groups for root growth, using either a good homemade blend of nutrients or a commercial feed (see Chapter 7, "Practical Pointers"). Although still dormant, spring-blooming bulbs will be awakening with the autumn rains, ready to begin their long, slow root growth. When you tidy the borders, collect ripe seed of summer onions and lily bulbils (the fat little proto-bulbs some lilies tuck into their armpits, just above the leaves). Sow these in deep (3–5 inches) flats or in the shallow pots called seed pans and let them winter over out of doors.

November

Early in the month, mow grass closely where true autumn and winter crocus will bloom. Tidy neighbors of fall bloomers so they have an attractive setting. Lift and prepare tender bulbs for winter storage. Prechill bulbs for forcing (see Chapter 6, "Bulbs in Containers"). Begin to feed and water amaryllis and other tender bulbs.

December

Pot up bulbs for forcing. Continue feeding amaryllis. If the weather has been mild, you may need to re-mow grass where snow crocus are to bloom.

January

Renew organic mulches around winter- and spring-blooming bulbs to reduce mud splash. As the first shoots appear, spread feeding mulches of alfalfa and compost. Indoors, give forcing pots more light. Increase water and begin to feed as active growth begins.

February

Continue spring feeding as more bulb shoots appear. Replenish moisture-conserving mulches around summer bloomers. As you tidy away winter weeds, watch for slug damage on new shoots. Bait only as needed, keeping bait close to the plants that need protection rather than broadcasting. Experiment to find the least toxic substances that are still effective (diatomaceous earth works beautifully).

March

Tidy fading foliage of the earliest bloomers, tucking browning leaves under mulch rather than braiding or removing them. Record your favorite combinations and effects in your garden journal and make notes about improvements you want to make next fall. Divide crowded snowdrops while their foliage is still green; reset at once in small clusters (3 to 5 bulbs, spaced 1 inch apart). Continue feeding forced bulbs, including amaryllis; remove flower stems and yellowing leaves, but keep adequately moist.

April

Continue to groom early bloomers as they ripen off. Plant pots of summer bulbs (lilies, gladiolas, and so forth). Remember not to mow the grass where crocus foliage is still ripening: you may have to wait till May to cut those patches.

May

Groom bulb foliage frequently but lightly to smooth the transition from spring into summer. Make sure that perennial companions haven't overgrown early-blooming bulbs—remember that they still need light and air even when dormant. Feed and slug-bait lilies. Check maturing crocus foliage; mow surrounding grass high the first few times.

June

Tidy or hide the last of the late tulip foliage under mulch. Remove yellowing leaves of autumn crocus (they look like huge, rotting cabbages) as they begin to go off. Collect seed of spring onions, fritillaries, and so forth. Sow in deep flats or seed pans and bait for slugs.

July

Remove all fully ripened bulb stems and foliage, covering their resting places with a mulch of compost and shredded bark or chopped straw. Groom summer bloomers and their companions. Order bulbs for fall planting, consulting your garden journal for ideas. Bring amaryllis outside for their summer baking.

August

Collect bulbils from Asiatic, tiger, and regal lilies. Sow in deep flats or seed pans (bait for slugs). Stop feeding amaryllis and begin to reduce their water. By month's end, they will be in full or partial dormancy. Bring indoors and store in light, warm place out of direct sunlight. Keep barely moist.

Index

(Bold page numbers indicate primary references.)

soil mixtures 53
See also Planting
Pre-soaking, for bulbs,
5, 11, 39, 42

Q–R

Quamash, 20, 48. *See
also Camassia*
Rain lily, 37, 77
Refrigerating bulbs for
forcing, 54–56
Regal lily, 26
Rhododendrons,6, 45,
47, 50, 66, 73
Ripening bulbs, leaves,
51, 69
Rock garden plants, 37
Rodent deterrents, 69,
70
Rosa
R. *rubrifolia*, 18
R. *rubrifolia* with
Regal lily, 26
Roses
Christmas, 79
rockrose (*Cistus* spp.),
22
winter, 79
with summer alliums,
17, 18
Rot prevention, 45, 57,
66, 67
Rubrum lily, 77

S

Sad Glads, 24
Sage, 3, 22, 49, 77
Scented varieties. *See*
Fragrant bulbs,
plants
Scilla, **44–45**
'Alba', 44
forcing, 54, 56
S. *bifolia*, 44

S. *bifolia* 'Rosea', 45
S. *sibirica, 38, 44
'Spring Beauty', 44
Sedums, 3, 8, 11
Seed collecting, 90, 91
Shrubs, 47, 50, 51, 73
Siberian iris, 48
Slug, snail protection,
69, 70, 91
Snow crocus, 4, 40, 79
Snowdrops, **42–43**
in border plantings,
38, 47, 50, 79
forcing, 54, 56
planting, dividing, 43,
90
Snowflake. *See* Autumn
Snowflake
Soil
amendments, 65, 66,
67, 68, 69
compost, 53, 65–67,
69
for container plant-
ing, 52, 53
mulching bulbs, 67,
68, 91
testing, guidelines, 65,
66
types, improvement,
65, 66
Sources for bulbs,
83–88
Southern Bugle Lily,
30–31
Squills, **44–45,** 54, 56
Squirrels, 69, 70
Staking tall bulbs, 28,
70
Sterilizing pots, soil, 53
Sunlight conditions, 46,
48, 50

T

Tender bulbs
autumn care, 55,
56–57, 91
container planting,
56–63
garden protection in
winter, 58
selection, 52, 59
winter storage, 57–58
Tiger Flowers. *See* Mex-
ican Tiger Flowers
Tiger lily, 17, **29**
Trillium
T. *chloropetalum*, 15
T. *gradiflorum*, 15
T. *ovatum*, 14–15
T. *sessile*, 15
Trilliums, 14–15
Triteleia. See Brodiaea
Trumpet lily, **28–29,**
70, 75
Tuberous begonia, 59,
60
Tulipa, **15–16**
T. *botalini* 'Bronze
Charm', 16
T. *clusiana*, 16
T. *pulchella* 'Violacea',
16
T. *tarda*, 16, 73
T. *turkestanica*, 16
Tulip, **15–16**
in borders, 10, 46, 47,
73
in containers, 53
Darwin types, 16
forcing, 56
lady tulip, 16
named varieties, 3, 12,
16, 39
rodent deterrents, 69,
70